D1604252

Shu

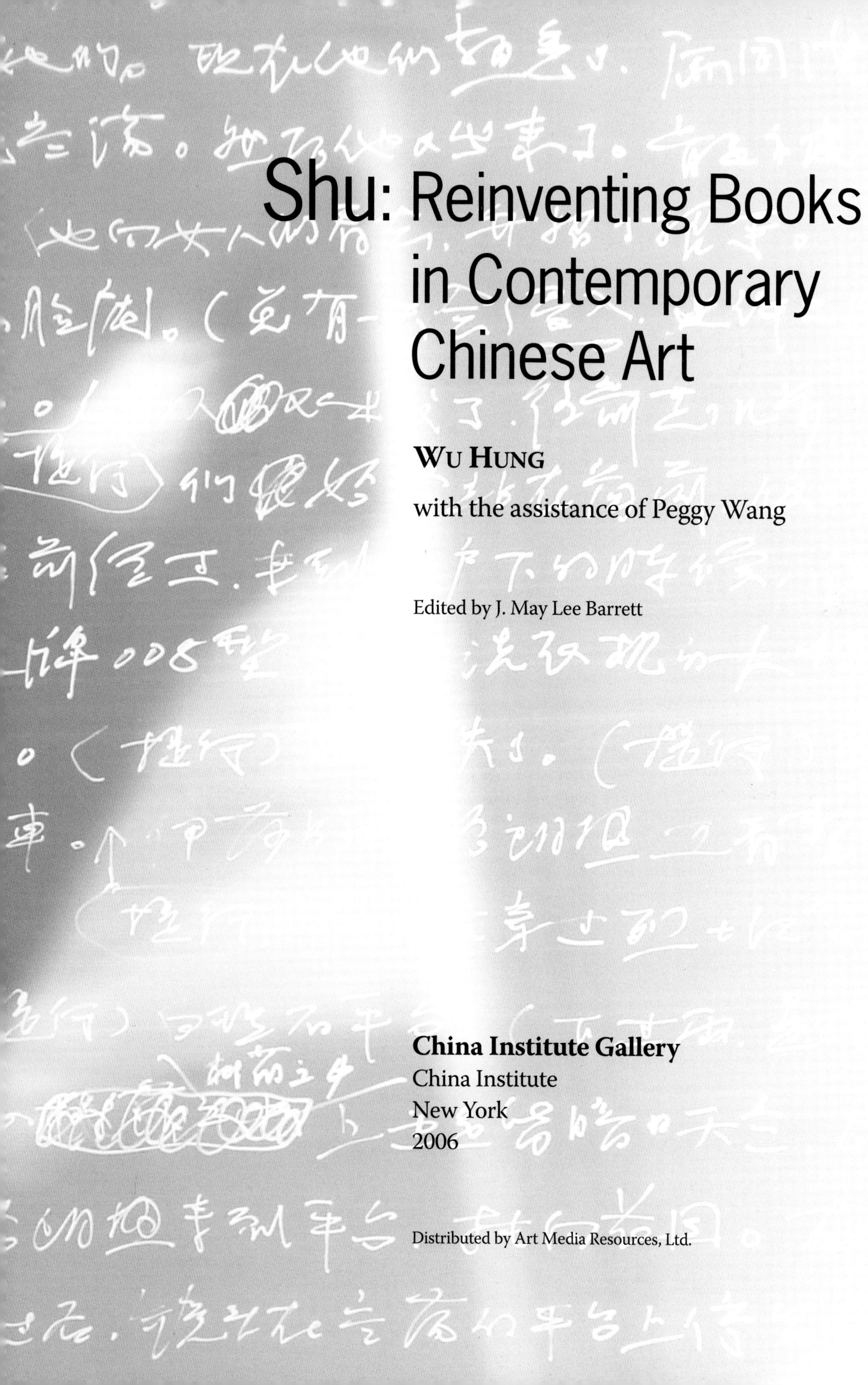

Shu: Reinventing Books in Contemporary Chinese Art

Wu Hung

with the assistance of Peggy Wang

Edited by J. May Lee Barrett

China Institute Gallery
China Institute
New York
2006

Distributed by Art Media Resources, Ltd.

China Institute Gallery
Celebrating 40 Years of Excellence
1966 ~ 2006

This catalogue was published to accompany the exhibition
SHU: REINVENTING BOOKS IN CONTEMPORARY CHINESE ART
To be held at ***China Institute Gallery*** in two parts:
Part I: September 28 – November 11, 2006
Part II: December 13 – February 24, 2007

China Institute Gallery
125 East 65th Street
New York, NY 10021
212.744.8181

Library of Congress Control Number: 2006931330
ISBN-10: 0-9774054-0-0
ISBN-13: 978-0-9774054-0-4

General Editor and Project Director: Willow Weilan Hai Chang
Editor: J. May Lee Barrett
Designer: Peter Lukic
Printer: Changsha Hongfa Printing Co., Ltd., China

The pinyin system of romanization is used throughout the text and bibliography except for the names of Chinese authors writing in Western languages. Chinese terms cited in Western-language titles remain in their original form and have not been converted.

China Institute was founded in 1926 by American philosopher John Dewey and Chinese educator Hu Shih, together with other prominent educators. It is the oldest bi-cultural and educational organization in the United States with an exclusive focus on China and is dedicated to promoting the understanding, appreciation, and enjoyment of Chinese civilization, culture, heritage, and current affairs through classroom teaching and seminars, art exhibitions, public programs, teacher education, lectures, and symposia.

Cover illustration (detail of pl. 40):
Wang Jin
New Ancient—Stele of Zhang Qian, 1998
Polyvinyl chloride (PVC)
Collection of the artist

Frontispiece and title page (detail of pl. 76):
Zhang Xiaogang
Written Memories, 2005
Photograph
Collection of the artist

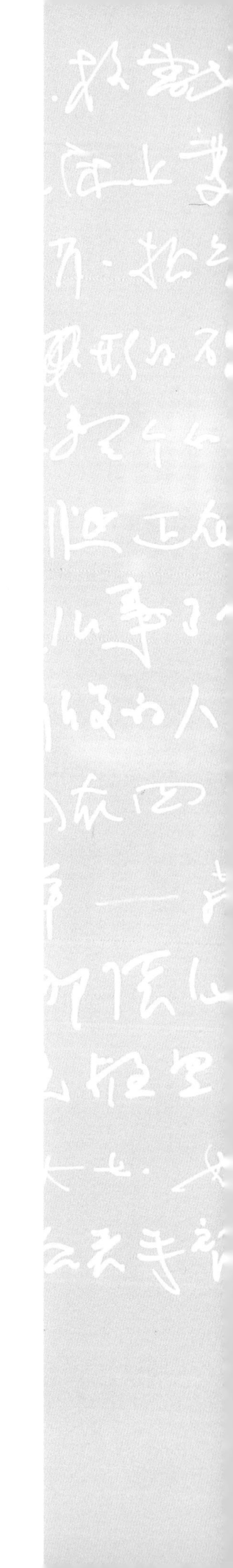

Contents

Sponsors of the Exhibition

*This exhibition, exhibition-related programming, and catalog have been made possible in part through the generous support of the following **

PATRONS

American Center Foundation
Fidelity Foundation
New York State Council on the Arts
W.L.S. Spencer Foundation

LEADERS

Changsha Hongfa Printing Co., Ltd., China
Continental Airlines
HSBC Bank, N.A.
Lily Auchincloss Foundation, Inc.
Martin Paskus Foundation, Inc.

CONTRIBUTORS

Susan L. Beningson, in memory of Renee Beningson
Christie's
Jane DeBevoise and Paul Calello
H. Christopher Luce and Tina Liu
Alice King
Museums Magazine
Robert Rosenkranz and Alexandra Munroe
Sophia Sheng
Larry Warsh

SUPPORTERS

Anita and Cyrus Tsui
Wood-Rill Foundation

INDIVIDUALS

John R. and Julia Curtis
Ivan Y. T. Feng Fund
Hart and Nancy B. Fessenden
Miani Johnson
Veronica Ogden
Theresa M. Reilly
Christopher Tsai
Marie-Hélène and Guy A. Weill
Yvonne L.C. Wong
Jonathan K. and Pearl T. Yu

We are also grateful for the continuing support to China Institute Gallery from

The Starr Foundation
China Institute's Friends of the Gallery

* At the time of printing

Lenders to the Exhibition

Chambers Fine Art
George Morton and Karol Howard
Hanart TZ Gallery
HSBC Bank, N.A.
Museum of Modern Art

Cai Guo Qiang
Gu Xiong
Hong Lei
Qin Chong
Qin Siyuan
Qiu Zhijie
Song Dong
Wang Jin
Wenda Gu
Xu Bing
Yuan Chin-t'a
Yue Minjun
Zhan Wang
Zhang Xiaogang

Message from the Chair of the Board of Trustees and the President of China Institute

To explore what China is today and where it may go in the future is essential to an understanding of global economics. Such an exploration is every bit as enlightening in the arts. We are pleased, therefore, to present *Shu: Reinventing Books in Contemporary Chinese Art* at the China Institute Gallery. It demonstrates an important new initiative at China Institute to expand our contemporary-themed exhibitions and programs.

While the works in *Shu: Reinventing Books in Contemporary Chinese Art* share the theme of books, they are more importantly the unique visual responses of individual artists to common issues. With this exhibition, China Institute Gallery fully engages itself with this remarkable generation and the question of what makes their art Chinese in the context of diaspora and Westernization. Some of these internationally known artists have chosen to pursue their careers outside China in such farflung places as New York, Paris, and Vancouver. A few were born and educated outside the People's Republic of China. Significantly, those still working in the PRC are indicators of the growing success of the avant-garde movement there. Over the past decade the Chinese avant-garde has developed a high profile in the international art scene, mirroring the rapid rise of China in the global economy. Contemporary Chinese art has come of age and cannot be ignored.

By broadening the scope of the Gallery's exhibitions to include a serious focus on current art movements in China, the Institute is afforded an opportunity to further the understanding among Americans of contemporary issues in Chinese society as well as the global nature of Chinese identity. We would like to thank the curator, Dr. Wu Hung, Harrie A. Vanderstappen Distinguished Service Professor of Art History, for sharing his profound insights on this subject. We would also like to thank China Institute Trustee Oscar L. Tang for his vision and encouragement in pursuing contemporary Chinese art initiatives. Also, our Gallery Director, Willow Weilan Hai Chang, and members of the Gallery Committee, past and present, merit our gratitude for their forward-looking vision in suggesting and promoting this exhibition. The success of this project is also a result of the continuing support of the Board of Trustees of China Institute, the Friends of the Gallery, and the Starr Foundation. We are also extremely grateful to the sponsors of the exhibition for their additional support, without which this project would not have come to fruition.

Virginia A. Kamsky
Chair, Board of Trustees

Sara Judge McCalpin
President

Foreword

One of the most common objects of our daily existence, books have for generations transmitted knowledge of human lives, wisdom, and experience, whether sorrowful or joyful. They are indeed among the best records of our civilization, past and present, and of our aspirations for the future.

In China the book is a venerated cultural icon, not the least because of its amazingly long history beginning with such ancient forms as inscribed oracle bones, bamboo strips, silk scrolls, and, after paper was invented in the Han dynasty, paper scrolls and albums. Books became especially widespread with the invention of movable type printing in the eleventh century. Most importantly, for a continuous period of over 1300 years lasting until almost the end of the Qing dynasty, the special Imperial Examinations System for selecting China's court officials fostered a broad reverence for books as well as for scholars. An old saying, "Spend ten years reading books near a cold window, then there will be a golden house and a jade-like beauty," reflects the allure of social and economic benefits for young men who study hard: passing the imperial examination could lead to a high official position with a handsome salary as well as the love of a great beauty.

Another expression, *shu ke hui ren, yi ke wu ren*, advises that while books could bring people fortune, it also could lead to less attractive consequences: for instance, those fettered by books or who live their entire lives reading books could turn into bookworms (*shudaizi*) or pedantic scholars (*furu*). But the Chinese have long felt that the power of books exceeds that of personal fortune to effect changes in the world. This is reflected, for instance, in the saying: *ban bu lun yu zhi tian xia* , or "with the knowledge from only half *The Analects* [a book citing the theories of Confucius as compiled by his students] you will govern the world well." *The Analects* did become the theoretical foundation of feudal rule in China for over a thousand years. Realizing that such power could be derived from books, regimes in various periods throughout Chinese history have imprisoned scholars for their writings (*wenziyu*) or banned books (*jinshu*). There are two well-known occasions in Chinese history when such a policy was carried out on a large scale: under the rule of Qin Shihuangdi (3rd century BCE) and, most recently, the decade-long period of the Cultural Revolution, which began in 1966. Like everyone else in China during those years, which were my formative years, I read the Little Red Book of Mao Zedong's sayings. I remember that aside from this we were permitted selected books on Communist subjects; most other books were banned.

An open-door policy followed upon the end of the Cultural Revolution in 1976, and China was soon flooded with books from everywhere on every subject: local and national, ancient and contemporary, east and west, man and woman, science and superstition, etc. This strong collision of subjects and ideas stirred complex feelings about books among the Chinese as they struggled to maintain their balance by adjusting their values and developing new aesthetic tastes. Now, moreover, they are also faced with a global environment and stimulating issues inside and outside the country. What then is their place in this environment?

Chinese artists were particularly sensitive to the rapid changes in society and the barrage of foreign ideas that they encountered in the last quarter of the twentieth century. The various avant-garde movements have endeavored with all earnestness to find a relevant place in the international art scene. At the same time it was a challenge to maintain a Chinese identity. The individual artists in this exhibition have used the book, both as subject and as medium, to express their concerns, their confusion, their aspirations, their disappointments, or their visions. Each of them, in their own way, invested this ancient Chinese cultural icon with contemporary concepts and sensibilities.

About three years ago, at the urging of the Board of Trustees to launch a contemporary Chinese art exhibitions, I approached Dr. Wu Hung to curate an exhibition, one that would link the traditional to the contemporary. His eyes brightened immediately, and he responded with a smile: "I have been thinking of this one subject for years; I think it will be very good for China Institute Gallery." That was the inception of this project, a moment that remains vivid in my memory.

Shu—Reinventing Books in Chinese Contemporary Art is the fruition of the vision that Dr. Wu so generously shared with China Institute. We are not only greatly indebted to him for curating this exhibition, but also for sharing his insights in the introductory essay. Our gratitude is extended to Peggy Wang, who assisted Dr. Wu by conducting the various interviews published in this catalogue. The artists in this exhibition merit our special thanks for agreeing to be a part of this project and for having created works that inspire us to see and experience the book in a new and different way.

We are indebted to the foundations and individual sponsors who have contributed generously to get this project off the ground and to make this vision a reality. I would also like to thank the Trustees of the China Institute and members of the Gallery Committee for their warm support of this new initiative. As always, I am very grateful to the loyal Friends of the Gallery for helping to make this exhibition possible and for their commitment to maintaining the high standards and reputation of the China Institute Gallery.

This project is also indebted to the many specialists who contributed their knowledge, talent, and energy to ensure its successful outcome. J. May Lee Barrett edited the catalogue and exhibition didactics with meticulous care and uncanny insight into matters of art and language. Perry Hu, our exhibition designer, overcame the challenge of our limited space and created what is in itself an exciting work of installation art. Under the pressure of an incredibly short deadline, Peter Lukic created an exceptional and inspired graphic design for this publication. Nicole Straus and Margery Newman promoted the exhibition in the media, bringing it to the attention of a wider audience.

As always, the entire China Institute staff is to be thanked for their patience and supportive assistance whenever the need arose. Regina Rodwell-Bell and her team assisted in the fund raising, and France Pepper arranged an interesting symposium for the exhibition. My sincere gratitude goes to the devoted gallery staff, Jennifer Choiniere and Pao Yu Cheng, for handling numerous and often difficult tasks necessary for the successful completion of the catalogue and mounting of the exhibition; to Ting Yuan for her assistance in translating the Chinese summary; and to the Gallery Docents and Volunteers for their unconditional and generous devotion. Finally, I would like to thank Sara Judge McCalpin, the President of China Institute, for her understanding and support.

Willow Weilan Hai Chang
Director
China Institute Gallery

Chinese Summary 中文简介

书在当代中国艺术中的再创

在过去的二十年间，中国前卫艺术家们创造出大量与“书”有关的作品，其不同凡响的出现频率和令人印象深刻的创造力都体现出“书”作为艺术想象和视觉词汇来源的重要性，同时展现了作为世界当代艺术分支的中国当代艺术的独到之处。

这个展览对“书”在中国当代艺术中的作用进行了首次严肃的考察，通过展出80年代中期以来中国当代艺术中的最重要的“艺术书籍”和以书为灵感的作品，反映了艺术家对中国当代艺术中的若干重大问题的思考，包括历史和文化记忆，东、西方关系，以及艺术家的自我身份。

展览包含两个连续部分，分别以“传统的重新想象”与“历史和记忆的协商”为主题，集中反映了中国当代艺术家们如何在其艺术实验中融入了自己对中国文化遗产与当代问题的思考，以及如何把自己对普遍性的社会和政治问题的回应，转化为高度个性化的艺术形象。

传统的重新想象

通过对装置、行为和多媒体等新艺术形式的应用，中国当代艺术家们得以摆脱二十世纪以来主要控制中国画坛的中、西二元模式。与油画和水墨画相比，当代艺术形式不具有强烈的文化属性。虽然上一世纪80和90年代中对这些形式的引进和使用，反映了当代艺术家颠覆国内旧艺术体制的强烈愿望，但这些形式并不构成与传统中国艺术或西方艺术的截然对立。它们为中国当代艺术家所提供的是一种“国际语”，使他们得以在国际舞台上探讨本土的问题。

中国当代艺术的这一特殊状态，解释了本次展览中作品的一个重要特点，即它们对国际艺术潮流和中国文化传统的同时切入。作为传统知识的主要媒介，“书”成为中国当代艺术家们重新发掘文化遗产和丰富其艺术实验的一个主要场地。这个展览中的不少作品吸取了传统中国书籍和书画艺术中的视觉元素，但是艺术家们并没有消极地固守流传久远的传统，而是发展出各种策略以质疑他们与往日中国的关系。他们的一个共同的策略，是对传统形式进行解构以表达新的概念和观点。另一个趋势则是用诸如录像和装置等当代艺术形式，来“翻译”传统书籍和册页。其结果是他们的作品强化了过去与现在之间的互动，也反映了艺术家们即希望保持传统又力图超越传统的愿望。

历史和记忆的协商

这一部分的展品大多源于艺术家们的亲身经历。对这些艺术家说来，“书”曾经最有力地唤醒他们对周围世界的好奇。他们童年时期的艺术天分也常常最先在手工制作的速写本中得到披露，在他们长大成人的过程中，他们的日记以及其他形式的个人记录记述了自己在文化大革命和其他政治运动中的私密记忆和创伤经历。这些记忆和经历使张晓刚、顾雄、徐冰、谢晓泽等艺术家创造出了他们饱含深情的作品。

其他的一些作品，则抨击了书在辅佐政治和宗教宣传中所扮演的角色，或讥讽了书在当代商业社会中每况愈下的知识价值——这两种态度都反映了对权威的否定和冷嘲。但是艺术家们的目的，并非是要简单地否定和毁弃书籍，而是希望以令人瞩目的新视觉形式，“出空”那些他们认为具有操纵性的、或是肤浅和赘述的书籍内容。陈心懋、耿建翌和岳敏君等艺术家的作品可以作为这种策略的代表，在拭去书中文字符号的同时创造出了新的视觉形式。

第三组作品对当今世界上的紧迫问题进行了反思。魏光庆、洪浩和蔡国强等艺术家运用书的不同形式，在其作品中对全球化、战争与和平以及东西方关系做出了评价。虽然这些是全人类所面临的重大部题，他们的作品的便携性和私密性强化了艺术家的独特的个人观点。

Shu: Reinventing Books in Contemporary Chinese Art

Wu Hung

"**READ THOUSANDS OF BOOKS**, travel thousands of miles" (*Du wan juan shu, xing wan li lu*) is a much repeated literary expression by modern Chinese artists in describing two main sources of their creative inspiration. Originally formulated by the Song neo-Confucian scholar Liu Yi (1017–1086) as a general prerequisite for a cultivated gentleman, it became linked with artistic learning through the influential Ming painter and theoretician Dong Qichang (1555–1636). In his *Notes from the Painting-Meditation Studio (Huachanshi suibi)*, Dong claims that the most essential quality of a good painting, known as "animation through spiritual consonance" (*qiyun shengdong*), is endowed by Heaven and cannot be acquired through human effort; what an artist can do is to "read thousands of books and travel thousands of miles," because in doing so he would "transcend the dusty and polluted world. Hills and valleys will naturally emerge in his mind and instantly form beautiful scenery like those of Juan and E. Freely expressing this with a brush, his work will be able to transmit the spirit of natural landsc ape."[1] Elsewhere, Dong wrote: "Without reading thousands of books and traveling thousands of miles, how can one become an original painter?"[2]

It is not until the early twentieth century, however, that "Read thousands of books, travel thousands of miles" became an essential maxim among Chinese artists. The reason for this unexpected development lies in the renewed significance of the expression. Whereas traditionalists used it to express their commitment to literati ideals,[3] modernists such as Xu Beihong (1895–1953) and Liu Haisu (1896–1994) connected it with their global experiences. Liu cited the idiom in an essay he wrote after traveling to Switzerland in 1929.[4] Xu used it when giving advice to the young Fu Baoshi (1904–1965), who in 1931 was still struggling to find new ways of thinking about painting: "Your achievement in depicting landscape is already quite remarkable and you should have a bright future as an artist. I would suggest that you study abroad to broaden your views. Read thousands of books and travel thousand of miles—you will surely become a great painter."[5] Following this advice, Fu went to Japan two years later to study studio art and art history.

Two reasons have prompted me to begin this introduction with a reflection on "Read thousands of books, travel thousands of miles." First, this popular expression demonstrates the extraordinary importance of the book to both traditional and modern Chinese artists. This importance can be explained from a number of perspectives. In terms of art criticism, throughout the history of Chinese painting, intellectual quality has remained a primary criterion in evaluating an artist's achievement. This quality cannot be acquired from artistic training alone, but has to be achieved through the artist's broad engagement with literature, philosophy, and history. Because books are principal sources of such knowledge, "reading" becomes mandatory to any artist unsatisfied with mere technical excellence.

In terms of artistic identity and practice,

painters since the emergence of scholarly painting in the Han dynasty have always played multiple roles in cultural production, not only as visual artists but also as poets, essayists, playwrights, and calligraphers. Their works often combine images and texts, and are subjects of both viewing and reading. After literati painting became the mainstream of Chinese art after the Yuan dynasty, the artistic persona implied in this practice grew into a standard model for all educated artists to follow. Finally, in terms of formal characteristics and reading/viewing conventions, books and paintings have much in common. For example, two major formats of traditional painting—the handscroll and the album—are also used for writing and printing books, and there are abundant books accompanied by exquisite illustrations, sometimes designed by famous painters. As a result of all these factors, paintings and books have enjoyed a unique relationship in Chinese culture, a relationship which is so fundamental to the artist that it has transcended enormous changes in Chinese art over the past two thousand years.

Second, the continuous currency of the expression "Read thousands of books, travel thousands of miles" in the twentieth century indicates an important aspect of modern Chinese art, which is its intense negotiation with China's cultural heritage. Indeed, it can be said that this negotiation played the most crucial role in shaping modern Chinese art as an independent twentieth-century artistic phenomenon with its own intrinsic logic and patterns of development. It is a shared understanding among art historians that the Westernization movement in Chinese art did not eliminate traditional art, but rather drew traditional art into a constant dialogue with it. As Michael Sullivan has observed, "In spite of the artistic controversies that enlivened the twenties and thirties, Chinese artists on the whole avoided the violent oscillations between acceptance and rejection of the West that had shaken Japanese art since the Meiji restoration of 1868."[6] Many of these artists took the "West" and the "past" as two parallel sources of styles as well as ideas, from which they could draw useful elements for creating a new type of Chinese art.[7] As "Read thousands of books, travel thousands of miles" was reconnected with this trend of thinking, Dong Qichang's age-old teaching obtained a new, modern meaning.

A similar pattern has been found in contemporary Chinese art since the 1980s: whereas the book maintains its importance to today's experimental artists,[8] its role in artistic creation has changed again. Most importantly, positioning themselves at the margin of mainstream Chinese culture, these artists have developed a complex love-hate relationship with the book. They recognize the bond connecting themselves with the book, but also attack the book for its manipulative power in politics and its banality in commercial culture. Moreover, contemporary art mediums, such as installation, video, and digital photography, have enabled these artists to "reinvent" books through a large number of book-related artistic experiments. The frequency of such projects during the past two decade is unparalleled in the world. Since these experiments betray no direct influence from Western art, they provide important evidence for understanding distinct characteristics of contemporary Chinese art and strongly refute a criticism repeated by official Chinese critics and some Western critics that experimental Chinese art as a whole is "derivative" and lacks indigenous roots.

This exhibition offers the first serious examination of this aspect of contemporary Chinese art. The more than thirty works in the show are selected from a large pool of examples and reflect a wide range of artistic experiments. The florescent forms and divergent thematic orientations of these works make one immediately aware of their originality. In fact, no two items in this show are alike. Some artists use books as ready-made materials; others have created unique books either as independent art objects or as components of large installations. Some artists deduce abstract concepts from traditional books; others have refashioned books into diverse, contemporary forms. Organized in two broad sections, these works substantiate "contemporary Chinese art"—a general and vague concept—with specific, individualized meaning.

Subtitled "Reimagining Tradition," the first section of the exhibition includes works that reflect the artists' desire to engage the past in a contemporary dialogue. A number of these works derive essential elements from traditional Chinese books and painting/calligraphy albums —including format, reading or viewing conventions, and painting and printing styles and materials. Instead of continuing established traditions passively, however, the artists have self-consciously developed different strategies to problematize their relationship with China's cultural heritage. A common strategy is to deconstruct traditional forms in order to express new concepts and ideas. Works in this section thus demonstrate a constant interaction between past and present, and between preservation and renovation.

The second section, "Negotiating History and Memory," is more closely related to the historical experiences of contemporary Chinese artists. Some works in this section are imbued with vivid personal memories of the Cultural Revolution; other works demonstrate a strong iconoclastic impulse, questioning the roles that books have played in standardized education and political propaganda. Several works in this section deal with urgent issues in today's world, including globalization, war and peace, and the relationship between East and West. This section also includes a site-specific project by the artist Qiu Zhijie. Surrounding a communal area outside the gallery spaces, it reminds the audience of the omnipresence of books in people's daily lives.

Instead of analyzing these works as isolated examples, the rest of this introduction will situate them within the historical context of post-Cultural Revolution China and connect them with several large issues, including historical and cultural memory, dialogue between past and present, the East-West relationship, self-identity of the artist, and pursuit of novel visual forms. Because these are among the most crucial and controversial issues in contemporary Chinese art, it is hoped that this discussion, as well as the artists' statements included in this catalogue, will contribute to a deepening understanding of this art as an important component of global contemporary art.

A New Beginning

The year 1987 witnessed the creation of two seminal works of experimental Chinese art: Huang Yong Ping's *"The History of Chinese Art" and "A Concise History of Modern Art" after Two Minutes in the Washing Machine* (fig. 1) and Xu Bing's *Book from the Sky* (fig. 2). Both employing books as central components, these two projects emerged at the height of the '85 Art New Wave (85 Yishu Xinchao), the first major contemporary art movement in post-Cultural Revolution China.

The '85 Art New Wave surfaced partly as a reaction to the Sixth National Art Exhibition held in 1984, which led to a direct confrontation between official and unofficial positions. Artists whose works were rejected by the government-sponsored exhibition criticized the exhibition committee for its unfair selection process and went on to hold their own show entitled *Exhibition of the Works which Have Failed to Enter the Sixth National Art Exhibition.* Numerous unofficial art groups appeared spontaneously in 1985 and 1986: according to one statistic, more than eighty such groups appeared across twenty-three provinces and major cities during these two years.[9] The members of these groups were mostly in their twenties; a considerable number of them had just graduated from or were still studying in art schools. Compared with earlier unofficial artists such as the members of the Stars Painting Society (Xingxing Huahui), this new generation of experimental artists were more knowledgeable about recent developments in Western art, and their opposition to official art was more radical, sometimes verging on iconoclasm. Their works, as well as their speech and writing, often consciously demonstrated an "avant-garde intent."[10] Following the mode of a *qunzhong yundong* (mass campaign), separate local groups soon joined together into a national network and began to envision a national exhibition of experimental art in the country's capital. But when the show, known in English as *China/Avant-garde*, finally took place in Beijing's National Art Gallery of China in 1989, it also marked the end of the '85 Art New Wave. Held in February that year, it anticipated the student demonstrations in Tiananmen Square two months later that ended in bloodshed.

When Xu Bing's *Book from the Sky* was shown in the National Art Gallery in October 1988, this enormous project was still only half completed; it was not until two years later that he would finish carving a total number of 4000 "fake characters" to print 400 books of nonsense texts. The composition, printing, and binding techniques of these books were strictly traditional (pl. 46–49). In the 1988 exhibition, multiple copies of the books lay on the floor in rows; their open pages formed, at least to one viewer, "a kind of metaphysical landscape, similar to a Zen garden or to a vast and unlimited plain or the sea from a bird's eye view."[11] Large paper sheets printed with the same characters covered a wall and hung from the ceiling, constituting a visual environment for the "sea of books." While the vertical sheets on the wall reminded people of traditional hanging scrolls, the graceful curve of the suspended long strips evoked the movement of horizontal handscrolls. A fourth component of the installation consisted of two sets of the *Book from the Sky*, including individual volumes and a wooden case. Placed on low platforms made of solid timber, each set bestowed the installation with a visual focus and a feeling of solemnity, "as if it were an altar with relics, or a commemorative gravestone."[12]

In comparison, Huang Yong Ping's *"The History of Chinese Art" and "A Concise History of Modern Art" after Two Minutes in the Washing Machine* involved no such painstaking effort to create artistic objects; in fact its purpose was to refuse any constructed system of knowledge by destroying the principal carrier of such knowledge—the book. Of the two volumes Huang machine-washed, the first was by the senior Chinese art historian Wang Bomin and had been used widely as a standard textbook in Chinese art schools; the second book, by American art historian Herbert Read, was well-known in the Chinese avant-garde circles in the 1980s, partly because it was one of the few introductions to modern Western art available at the time in Chinese translation. Putting these two books through a two-minute wash cycle in a washing machine, Huang Yong Ping produced a pile of paper pulp—the remains of the books—which he then displayed on a broken glass panel atop a used wooden box. According to him, this was his response to an enigmatic question that had preoccupied generations of modern Chinese intellectuals and artists: how to position oneself between tradition and modernity and between East and West? Instead of providing another idealistic solution, Huang's installation challenges the premise of the question by eliminating the binary concepts. The paper pulp, as the joined remains of the two books, can be considered an art product that erases the conventional dichotomy between tradition and modernity and between East and West.

Since their first exhibitions in 1988 and 1989, these two works have attracted wide attention both in China and abroad. Art critics now generally consider them among the most important examples of contemporary art from the 1990s, not just in China but also in the world. Pablo J. Rico, for example, wrote in 2004 about the *Book from the Sky* as "a work which, following several presentations in China, Japan and the United States, was eventually exhibited at the 45th Venice Biennale (1993) to critical acclaim, bringing Xu Bing widespread recognition as one of the most singular artists of his generation."[13] As for Huang Yong Ping's installation, Fei Dawei recently claimed that "it is not only a milestone in contemporary Chinese art but also a rare international contemporary art masterpiece."[14]

Fig. 1. Huang Yong Ping (1954–), "*The History of Chinese Art*" *and* "*A Concise History of Modern (Western) Art*" *After Two Minutes in the Washing Machine*, 1987. Installation; wood, glass, pulped books, and ink; 29.2 x 73 x 28.6 cm (11½ x 28¾ x 11¼ in.). Photograph of original installation

Few writers, however, have talked about a central element in these two works: the book. Why did Xu Bing spend years to make hundreds of elegant but unreadable volumes? Why did Huang Yong Ping choose two popular textbooks as the subject of destruction? An investigation of the two artists' careers shows that their interests in books were neither random nor coincidental, but were related to their personal experiences as well as their views of culture and society at large. Xu Bing recalled his childhood memory in an interview conducted for this exhibition:[15]

> My generation has a very awkward relationship with words and books. In my personal

> experience, for example, I grew up in a culturally rich environment because of my parents' employment. Both of my parents worked at Beijing University, so I spent a lot of time at the library there. Because they were often very busy, they would let me stay in the library stacks. I was very young at that time, though, and I couldn't read any of the books. I would just page through the reference books, for example, texts on bookbinding, calligraphy styles, typesetting, the history of books, etc. I would also look at the different ways in which books were bound. I became very familiar with the books' exteriors, although I didn't know any of their contents. By the time of the Cultural Revolution, I could read, but there weren't any books available. The entire country read only one book: Mao's "Little Red Book." We read and memorized that book all day. At the end of the Cultural Revolution, I returned from the countryside to Beijing to study. Because I was starving for culture and was in the midst of the general cultural fever at the time, I read so many different types of books. But after reading so much, I didn't feel well. It was like being overstuffed. It was at that time that I made the *Book from the Sky.* It's the very awkwardness of this relationship with books and words that drew my interest to this subject.[16]

Such a personal relationship with the book explains why so many of Xu Bing's projects have focused on this artifact—not only on text and script but also on the form and materiality of the book. These works include *A, B, C...* (1991), *Post Testament* (1992), *Wu Street* (1993), *Cultural Animal* (1993–94), *A Case Study of Transference* (1994), *Silkworm Book* (1994–95), *Introduction to Square Work Calligraphy* (1994) (pl. 50–51), *Body Outside Body* (2000), and the many "books" in the *Tobacco Project* (2000) (pl. 53–60). Although each work has its specific purpose, a common tendency running through these projects can be summarized as a simultaneous destruction and construction of books. We can again trace this tendency to the *Book from Sky.* While it violates a thousand-year-long Chinese literary convention by making the book incomprehensible, it also derived the means to enact this violation from the Chinese cultural tradition. These means—woodblock carving and book printing—mimic the formative process of Chinese literary culture, and in Xu Bing's art they become the primary sites of meaning.[17]

In Huang Yong Ping's case, *"The History of Chinese Art" and "A Concise History of Modern Art" after Two Minutes in the Washing Machine* was also one of his many book-related art projects dating from the 1980s and 1990s. This corpus of works started out from a project entitled *A Book Collection* in 1984. In that year he traded one of his paintings with a foreign student for a copy of *The Story of Modern Art.* He then glued the book together page by page, "turning it into a brick in order to 'lock up' modern art history."[18] Thus, he had already developed a radical "anti-art history" attitude three years prior to *"The History of Chinese Art" and "A Concise History of Modern Art" after Two Minutes in the Washing Machine.* Approaching the history of art as a process of competition, control, and holocaust, he had also found a basic means to counter this history of control by "containing" standard art historical books, either locking them up or washing them with water.

According to Huang Yong Ping himself, he made his first "book washing" project in early 1987 in his home in Xiamen: "I put the books from the bookshelves into the washing machine and switched it on, then put the entire pulp mixture back onto the shelves" (fig. 1). While this experiment led to the creation of *"The History of Chinese Art" and "A Concise History of Modern Art" after Two Minutes in the Washing Machine* later that year, the latter project was again followed by *A Humid "Critique of Pure Reason"* in 1988, in which he washed Immanuel Kant's *Critique of Pure Reason* and *Book Cabinet.* After Huang emigrated to France in 1989, his large-scale performances/installations continued the "book washing" theme. These projects included *Reptile* (1989, Centre Georges Pompidou, Paris), *Should We Construct Another Cathedral?* (1991, Galerie

Fenster, Frankfurt), *Unreadable Humanity* (1991, Carnegie International, Pittsburgh), *House of Oracles* (1992, Galerie Froment & Putman, Paris), *Library Canteen* (1992, Bibliothèque Forney, Paris), *Kiosk* (1995), and *Floating Kiosk* (2000, Musée Moderne de la Ville de Paris). While all these projects featured the destruction of books as a symbolic gesture to subvert established systems, the decision to stage such destructions in prominent Western cultural institutions signified Huang's intensified desire to challenge the dominance of eurocentrism.

Although brief, this discussion of Xu Bing and Huang Yong Ping's book-related projects demonstrates a central role for the book in contemporary Chinese art. It also reveals four fundamental concepts or paradigms which are crucial not only to understanding these two artists, but also to interpreting the contemporary Chinese artists' general engagement with books. The first is an artist's intimate relationship with books through personal experience and memory. The second is the significance of books to collective ideology and cultural identity. The third is the formal and technical features of books as sources of artistic imagination and creativity. The fourth is the role of books in the interlocution between past and present and between local and global. These concepts intersect with each other, providing contemporary Chinese artists with a broad basis to conduct wide-ranging artistic experiments which address artistic, intellectual, political, and personal issues.

OBJECT OF INTIMACY

For this exhibition we have interviewed many invited artists. Although we anticipated they would connect their works with personal experiences, we have nevertheless been surprised by the richness of their reminiscences about the roles that books have played at different stages in their lives (see the artists' statements in this catalogue). It seems that the topic of the "book" opened a hidden door, allowing them to speak about their art in a personal, intimate voice. Earlier I cited Xu Bing's description about how as a young kid he was initiated into the world of books in the stacks of the Beijing University Library. Zhang Xiaogang, another leading contemporary Chinese artist, also developed a "book complex" early on, as he recounts in an interview:

> Since my childhood, I have loved reading books and buying books. When I was young, however, some books were very hard to come by, so we had a habit of making handwritten copies. This practice also functioned as a learning process. I think my affection for books must also be related to the '85 Art New Wave movement; during that period of time, everyone loved to read. In my mind's eye, then, books are sacred but also dangerous. There was also a period, beginning in the 1990s, when I hated books—I felt that they were useless. In a way, this has to do with the fast-paced changes in China: there's no longer any time to read, particularly Western literature or philosophy. Books are our friends, but sometimes they are our demons. I harbor such contradictory feelings towards books: on the one hand I am very suspicious of them, and on the other hand I can't be without them.

Although Zhang Xiaogang is best known for his oversized portraits of anonymous figures during the Cultural Revolution, this autobiographical account strikes at a deeper core in his art: books became central images in his paintings long before the portraits and have recently returned to his repertoire in a series of "visual diaries" called *Amnesia and Memory*. It is true that he has also depicted other daily objects such as the telephone, the television, a knife, a burning candle, a flashlight, etc., either for their sentimental value or for their symbolic significance, but none of these images are more frequent and consistent than books. The reason is that, as he reveals in the interview, books best encapsulate his ambivalence toward himself and the world. In many of his paintings dating from the late 1980s to early 1990s, books stood for admonition and repression but were also imbued with deep emotion. This dual significance of books is related to his personal crisis at the time as well as the tragedy of the June Fourth Movement.[19] A series of paintings shown in this exhibition, titled *Private Notes* and executed in watercolor and oil on paper, is an important example from this period. The seven compositions in the 1991 series constitute a metaphorical diary over a week; a numbered calendar on the back wall indicates the sequence of the seven days (pl. 65–71). Books and dismembered body parts are two central motifs in the compositions, interacting with each other in various ways to suggest a continuing narrative. These images—a yellowish hand holding a pen to write on a piece of paper, a red hand pointing at a sentence in a book, a broken arm laying on pages covered with tiny characters—seem to convey traumatic experiences and signify yearning and desperation; their dark mood conflates memories of the Cultural Revolution and the June Fourth Movement.

The strong symbolic overtone of *Private Notes* continues to characterize *Genesis*, which Zhang Xiaogang created in 1992. The two paintings in this mini-series depict two newborn babies in the center, each lying above a desk next to an open book. One baby is reddish and raises his head to stare into the onlooker's eyes. The other baby is yellowish and turns his head toward the book, reading the text under the guidance of a disembodied red hand. Old photos painted in the background offer clues for understanding the meaning of each composition. The photos on the top row behind the first baby represent Communist pioneers, including the founders of the Chinese Communist Party. The baby may thus symbolize the original inspiration of the revolution and the awakening of the Chinese people—a significance reinforced by the baby's alertness and "revolutionary" color. The photos in the other painting show "revolutionary students" during the Cultural Revolution, either marching in mass rallies or being re-educated through labor in the countryside. The passive and obedient baby in front of these pictures seems to typify the experience of this generation, which received Communist ideology as unfeeling dogma dictated by an impersonal, faceless power.

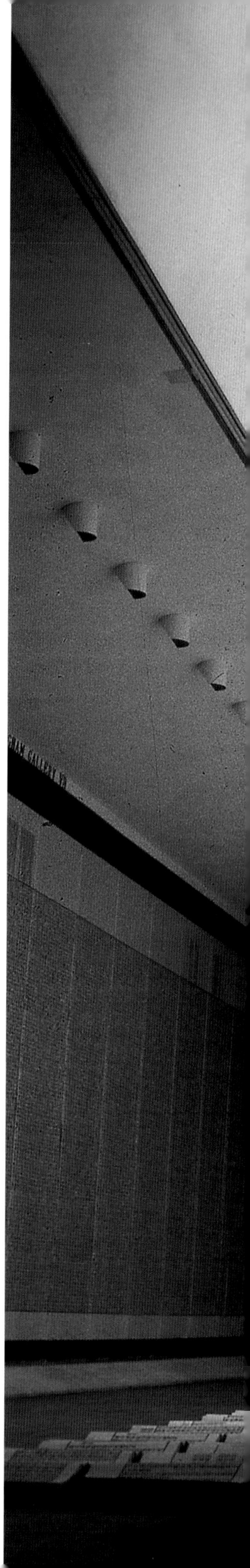

Fig. 2. Xu Bing (1955–), *Book from the Sky*, 1988. Photograph of installation

What one finds in these paintings, therefore, are "memory images" resurrected from history and from the depth of the artist's psyche. Influenced by Surrealism and Expressionism, Zhang Xiaogang devised a private iconography, in which the book stands for bygone experiences as well as a persistent dilemma in the present.[20] Gu Xiong's work in this exhibition exemplifies a different mode of intimacy with books: instead of representing memory, it preserves history in its original form (pl. 7–16). The work consists of a series of sketchbooks, handmade by the artist during the Cultural Revolution when he was sent to a mountainous area in southwest China to receive re-education. Day after day, month after month, he covered the pages of the sketchbooks with drawings of revolutionary heroes and heroines, figures and stories in newspapers, and people and things surrounding him. To a researcher of the Cultural Revolution, these sketchbooks offer a rare body of materials to understand the prevailing visual culture during that period: unlike propaganda posters issued by the government, these were created by a teenage amateur artist for self-fulfillment and reflected his private visual sensibility. In an interview, Gu Xiong recalled his experience at the time and explained why he had decided to make facsimiles of the sketchbooks for this exhibition: only when the audience actually "touches" these books can they share his intimate feeling towards them.

> I went from the excitement of the Cultural Revolution to the remote countryside and began to reflect on the conditions of the revolution. Despondency about the realities of my life and the unpredictability of the future lingered and went back and forth in my mind. These all compelled me to draw. Every morning, I would carry my sketchbooks with me. When we took a break from physical labor, I would pull them out and draw images of the peasants or the scenery. At night, I would sit under a kerosene lamp and recollect my experiences from the day. I would find what was meaningful from that day and draw it. In those four years, I produced about twenty or so sketchbooks...
>
> At the time that I made these sketchbooks, they were a way of recording reality. I think that the book, particularly if you make it yourself, is an extremely individual and unique format. When this personal format reaches the public, even if the audience has had different experiences, it will still resonate with them. When you touch a book, you can really feel that it has existed in history, in a cultural space. You can pick it up and take part in some of its temporal and spatial experiences. Even if I make a new copy of a sketchbook for viewers to touch, it will itself become a meaningful work. It will no longer be a piece just for me, but will be something used and read by a broader public. When it returns to me, it will have been transformed.

Interestingly, when Gu Xiong's drawings are reproduced for this exhibition in their original format, they will change their identity from private records of an artist's inner dialogue to public reading materials—from sketchbooks to books.

"Intimacy" also offers a key to understanding several other works in this exhibition, including Qin Siyuan's (Colin Chinnery) *A Self-Portrait Book* (pl. 37), Liu Dan's *Dictionary* (pl. 30), Xiaoze Xie's *Chinese Library No. 1* (pl. 45), and Yuan Chin-t'a's *Piling Up Books* (pl. 62). Each page of Qin Siyuan's *A Self-Portrait Book* shows a photographic detail of the artist's body and face, and the pages all together make up a complete image of his body and face. A portrait as a spatial art form is therefore transformed into a temporal representation, and the conventional way of "viewing" a portrait is channeled into a sequential "reading" of fragmentary facial and bodily features. As I will discuss later in this introduction, the intrinsic temporal quality of the book has inspired many contemporary Chinese artists to conduct art experiments. Qin Siyuan's *A Self-Portrait Book* is special in combining the experiences of "reading" and "touching": while turning the pages, the viewer must physically touch the images. ("There's a kind of intimacy to it," Qin says in an interview, "but also a slightly strange sensation.") To enhance such a sensation, he made the book with a special kind of *xuanzhi*—a traditional Chinese paper which is supple and soft, and has a texture similar to skin. He also insists that unlike a rarified art object, this book should be handled by viewers without gloves on. Although such physical contact will unavoidably damage the work, this will only prove its identity as a real book.

Whereas Qin Siyuan transformed a still image into a book, Liu Dan turns a book into an iconic image (pl. 30). The central concept remains intimacy, however. Measuring 230 by 330 centimeters, Liu's painting in this exhibition magnifies an old dictionary to a monumental scale. Interestingly, several artists have mentioned their special feeling toward dictionaries. Among them, Qiu Zhijie's account best articulates such an attraction:

> The book that has had the greatest impact on me has been the dictionary. Ever since I was a child, I've repeatedly read the dictionary... Reading classical dictionaries allows you to trace your origins; you feel like you can see the most fundamental things. When you're done reading, it's like you've discovered everything, as if the whole world were only composed of these things.

Like the natural world, a dictionary offers raw materials—words and definitions, not digested discourses and narratives. Reading a dictionary resembles exploiting a mine or excavating an archaeological site, activities which evoke the feeling of "going down to the bottom," of making original discoveries and regaining one's roots. We can thus understand why this type of book is especially favored by avant-garde artists, who by nature resist both canonical teaching and common wisdom. Indeed, the dictionary is arguably the most important type of book in the world and also has the longest shelf life, as one can never finish "reading" a dictionary but will endlessly return to it for help. Liu Dan's painting captures all these sensibilities. By enlarging an ordinary dictionary hundreds of times its original size, he bestows it with the status of a monument. By depicting the dictionary with a painstaking, photorealistic style, he stresses its vulnerability to time and to human touch: the book's yellowish paper and worn pages arouse nostalgia, testifying probably to a life-long intimate relationship with a human subject.

Against the Book

But do all the artists in this exhibition approach books as intimate objects invested with personal memory? The answer is clearly "no." In fact, several works emphasize a meaning of the book that is entirely opposite to intimacy. Instead of attaching sentimental values to books, their creators display various negative attitudes—suspicion, cynicism, iconoclasm—toward books. An implicit argument shared by these artists is that because books are made by men, they cannot avoid being used by political and religious authorities to advance their ambitions. A grave lesson these artists learned from the Cultural Revolution is exactly the alarming capability of a single set of books to control millions of people. Books are full of lies and are also battlegrounds of different politics, religions, and ideologies. This dark side of the book is the central theme of Wei Guangqing's *Black Covered Book: Desert Storm* (pl. 41). The book is entirely black. A metal instrument on its open left-hand page contains photographs of Saddam Hussein and George Bush, commanders in chief of the first Gulf War. Miniature warriors and military vehicles are scattered around, covering the rest of the pages. Fifteen years after this book's creation, we can now better appreciate the artist's prophetic vision: as the revived war in Iraq drags on, this "black book," made in 1991, continues to comment on current international politics.

Many contemporary Chinese artists also attack books for their "contamination" of culture. In their view, most books are commercial items disguised as educational tools. A majority of books, especially best-sellers, are empty in content and poor in taste. Still many other books cannot even realize their commercial value, as they travel directly from production lines to waste stations, leaving no impact on society. It is clear that in making such judgments, these artists are actually commenting on the general conditions of contemporary culture; but the book offers them a sharp focus to deliver such criticism. Their arguments also imply that they are not opposed to *all* books. In fact, their rage and sarcasm is often induced by their care for books. This seemingly contradictory attitude is revealed by several interviews, in which the artist abruptly shifts from condemning books to revealing his debt to them (a typical example is Yue Minjun's statement in this catalogue). When using art to attack those books they consider manipulative, shallow, or superfluous, their typical strategies include ridiculing them, exposing their emptiness, and rendering them meaningless. We have observed these tendencies in Xu Bing's *Book from the Sky* and Huang Yong Ping's *"The History of Chinese Art" and "A Concise History of Modern Art" after Two Minutes in the Washing Machine.* Several other examples in this exhibition further demonstrate the wide variety of art experiments made along these lines.

Yue Minjun's *Garbage Dump* ridicules books (pl. 63). Combining sculptures and ready-made materials, it shows six identical figures squatting in a circle, staring at a pile of books while laughing hysterically. Yue purchased the books from a refuse station. These books include philosophical treatises and textbooks on various subjects, popular literature and how-to-do manuals, and many other kinds. Some of them were used, but many have never been opened. The only factor that unites them is their shared identity as trash. To Yue Minjun, this random collection of books "hints at the enormous amount of cultural garbage present in modern society, all of which work to bind and fetter people's spirits."

The six squatting figures are all based on the artist's own physiognomy and can thus be considered self-portraits. Instead of contemplating the books, they exude a kind of frenzied excitement that is at odds with the context. Yue Minjun says that he deliberately juxtaposes the books with this image of himself, which "is the exact opposite of those images that one always sees of scholars and their attitudes towards books." The real subject of the work is therefore the self-representation of the artist. In fact, one can easily imagine the installation would maintain its basic meaning even if other objects replaced the books, because what the figures are laughing at are not just books, but the entirety of contemporary culture.

This mode of self-representation originated in Cynical Realism—a style that became popular in contemporary Chinese art around the early 1990s and was first exemplified by Fang Lijun's skin-head youth with a gaping yawn on his face. Like Fang's distorted self-image, Yue Minjun's figures encapsulate a dilemma faced by a generation of Chinese artists. As Li Xianting has noted, these artists "have lost faith in the dominant ideology, but also have no intention of making any effort to oppose this ideology and replace it with a new one. Finding no way out, they have developed a practical and self-serving attitude. Boredom is the most effective means of these cynics to free themselves from any shackle of responsibility."[21] These artists, however, have made an important contribution to contemporary Chinese art in forging an "iconography of self-mockery." In a sense, the distorted face in this iconography is a mask—a "false facade" (C: *jiamian* or *mianju*) as a means of both performance and disguise. If Yue Minjun's figures are still self-portraits, what they portray is no longer a real human subject but an autonomous figure. Encountering the pile of books, the figures' exaggerated excitement only masks the artist's true feeling towards these objects. As he continues in the interview: "Books are very important to my production process… [But] to extract from this immense tide of books the meaningful ones, the ones that you rely on your own consciousness to understand, is extremely difficult."

Yue Minjun's visual strategy is reversed by Wang Jin in his *New Ancient – Stele of Zhang Qian* (pl. 40).

Instead of juxtaposing real books with a distorted self-image, Wang distorts books to expose their identity as mechanical productions. His method is to use PVC, a transparent, durable industrial material, to copy delicate ink rubbings bound in a traditional book format. He explains:

> There are so many books today that cannot be read. Books are an industry, and reading them isn't important. Reading a book is like eating a hamburger. It's okay not to eat a hamburger, and it's okay not to read. This is not a society that needs or depends on books...
>
> Books are also extremely stubborn. Even if you don't read them, they are still there, challenging you. Books have a certain ambience about them. Even without reading a book, you can feel it. It's like a magnetic field. I feel that the natural properties of PVC and books are very similar. They are both stubborn. They will not decay over the course of hundreds of years. Wood, metal, and paper will deteriorate over time, but PVC will not. It might change in color or texture, but it will still be there. Books, too, possess these properties of preservation and continuity.

Wang Jin's *Stele of Zhang Qian* cannot be read or used for studying ancient calligraphy; instead it resembles a three-dimensional sculpture which can only be appreciated visually. We can "see through" the pages from cover to cover and observe the overlapping layers of words. His PVC book thus does not merely illustrate his statement that "books are an industry," but translates sarcasm into artistic imagination. This strategy of simultaneously destroying and reinventing visual forms is employed by several other artists in the exhibition. For example, each character in Geng Jianyi's *Misprinted Books* is formed by superimposing layers of characters (pl. 4). As such, these books dispel any idea of significance, and, in Johnson Chang's words, "play havoc with the traditional notion that a book is a record of valuable information."[22] When these books were first shown in the *China's New Art, Post-1989* exhibition in 1993, they appeared together with a group of three paintings based on popular images during the Cultural Revolution. In the central composition, Geng Jianyi painted the head of a giant panda inside the circle of a Red Sun—the place reserved for Mao's portrait. Paired with this painting, the *Misprinted Books* had a strong political implication as the artist's blasphemy of the sacred doctrine of the Party. But even in that context, the work still evoked formal appreciation, as the lines after lines of misprinted characters assumed an aesthetic quality, generating a visual rhythm with a hypnotic power.

Chen Xinmao's *History Book Series–Blurred Printing* also features distorted texts—incomplete and partially smeared woodblock prints as a result of misprinting (pl. 3). The blurred characters appear dilapidated, as if "ruins" or "traces" of some canonical books from the past. According to the artist, the basic concept of the work is that "over thousands of years the transmission of texts has led to the deterioration of meaning." Ironically, the distortion of historical texts in these images provides a means to explore new visual sensibility. The ambiguity between textual and visual expression is further heightened by the varied use of ink, which assumes contradictory roles: reproducing texts and making texts illegible, sometimes used to print characters and sometimes burying characters under richly-textured, spreading blots.

We may say that these works all reveal an effort to "empty" the content of the book for the sake of making art. Thus Wang Jin created his "transparent" volumes of ink rubbings, and Geng Jianyi and Chen Xinmao made their paintings and installations with the "misprinted" texts. Song Dong designed *A Room of Calligraphy Model Books* for a similar purpose (pl. 39). He used scissors to cut the pages of calligraphy model books into strips. Assembling the destroyed volumes into a "carpet" on the floor under running electric fans, he created an impression of wind blowing on a grass field of ink rubbings. In making this installation he was inspired by a tragic event in Chinese history in which a scholar during the Qing was put to death because he wrote this poetic couplet: "Gentle wind, you cannot read, so why do you turn the pages" (*Qingfeng bushizi, hebi luan fanshu*)? Because the character *qing* was also the name of the dynasty, the Emperor suspected that the couplet was a slur against his regime.

This historical episode seems to capture Song Dong's ambivalence toward the book, which transmits knowledge but does not guarantee its authenticity. Unlike the inscription on a stone stele, he argues, the rubbings reproduced in a calligraphic model book only offer fragmentary signs; the act of copying them can hardly help people understand the original text. He said in a recent interview: "I didn't shatter the stone into pieces. It is the publication of its rubbings that needs to be reformed. Over the years, people have copied these rubbings. Some people become geniuses, but most are circumscribed by tradition." Such suspicion toward received knowledge must have deep roots in his thinking, because his first public exhibition in 1994 already aimed to "empty" books. Called *One More Lesson: Do You Want to Play with Me?*, this exhibition transformed the gallery into a classroom, in which some students were reading wordless textbooks. The local authorities canceled the show the day it opened.

The notion of a "wordless book" has never left Song Dong, however. In the interview, he disclosed that his favorite book actually has only blank pages, and that he has been reading this book now and then since 1994. The same idea must have also inspired his *Water Diary*, in which he writes words everyday on a slab of stone with a brush dipped in pure water. Hong Hao's *Mexico-Huun-Amate* offers another example of a wordless book in contemporary Chinese art (pl. 17). Completely devoid of text, it seems to only feature empty pa ges of coarse paper. Upon minute examination, however, one finds that the fibers on the pages are actually painted by the artist with a tiny brush, and the paper's "handmade" quality actually results from pictorial illusionism. The book is therefore both absent and present. Or, the absence of its literary content leaves the viewer to concentrate on its visual and material presence.

Like Xu Bing, Zhang Xiaogang, and Song Dong, Hong Hao has been a dedicated "book artist" since the 1980s. This is not to say that he has dedicated himself to making "art books" during these years. Rather, the idea of the "book" has stayed in the center of his art experiments, whether he is making prints, photographs, or actual books. His first group of "book images" represented art catalogues. He explains that at the time he was very impressed by imported catalogues, which "seemed to symbolize a level of achievement." While still a student in the Printmaking Department in the Central Academy of Art, Beijing, Hong Hao found a way to attain such glory and satirize his own vanity: he made a series of *trompe l'oeil* prints of art catalogues that featured his works.

This early series paved the way for *Selected Scriptures*, a large collection of prints which took Hong Hao twelve years to realize. In a sophisticated illusionistic style, each print represents a picture in a large encyclopedia; its page number indicates its position in the book (pl. 18–21). The encyclopedia, however, remains a mental construct and is never realized in a material form. The diverse subjects of the prints/illustrations, the random use of multiple languages, and the heterogeneous origins of pictorial motifs further defy any rational structure and coherent layout. The meaning of this book lies in its illogicality. Hong Hao knows this better than anyone else:

> We use books for specific purposes. When we go to the library or bookstore, we look for books that we need. If you're looking to learn a foreign language, you will buy a foreign language textbook. Here, however, I have taken away the functionality and contextual continuity of the book. Although all of these pages are supposedly from one book, you don't actually know what this book is about. In real books, the first page is

related to the second page, etc. In my book, however, the contents of each page are independent of each other. I've revised the structure so there is no longer a sense of continuity. Although I've used the format of the book, I've taken away what one thinks a book should be. This book can't be used to find answers. This same principle applies to the maps: the longer you use them, the more confused you will become. I spent about twelve years, from 1988 to 2000, to make prints for this book.

Ironically, as "illogicality" is taken as a serious goal of art making, it begins to produce a "logic" to understand Hong Hao's various projects. Planning an exhibition of his new works in 2004, he conceptualized the gallery as a fictional reading room in which every book made by him would challenge normal "reading" in a unique way.[23] When the exhibition opened, it appeared as a laboratory of "anti-books." There was the *Mexico-Huun-Amate* with painted fibers on its empty paper. Another book called *AiA* was created by eliminating components from a published book, hence the meaning of this work in the form of an incomplete copy of an issue of *Art in America*. A third book combines images scanned or removed from several hundred books. While none of these images are related in content, they were carefully arranged by Hong Hao on opposing pages according to certain "visual codes" of a conventional catalogue. The book is neither readable nor unreadable. Its authorship is equally blurry. "Catalogues abide by certain standards and rules," Hong Hao announces, "but mine defy the function, structure, and production expected of books."

Negotiating Tradition

Throughout the twentieth century, a Chinese painter had to choose between the traditional medium of ink on paper and the "Western" medium of oil on canvas. He had to make such a choice because twentieth-century Chinese painting was predicated on the dichotomy between *guohua* (national painting) and *xihua* (Western painting), which determined the structure of education, the criteria of art criticism, and the artist's professional identity and self-image. This dichotomy also provided a basis for a persistent debate around two questions: How can "national painting" be modernized and "Western painting" become Chinese? Answers were sought in both theory and practice, but rarely challenged the dichotomy itself. An oil painter might derive aesthetic principles and technical elements from traditional art, and an ink painter might enrich his work with color and shading. But they were still *youhua* (oil painting) and *guohua* painters. Some artists tried to cross the boundary by making both types of painting, but this only demonstrated their ambidextrous skills, not a dismantling of the system.

This situation changed in contemporary art. With the introduction of new art forms in the 1980s and 1990s, contemporary Chinese artists have finally transcended the dichotomy of *guohua* and *xihua*. This is because compared with oil and ink painting, these contemporary art forms—installation, performance, site-specific art, multi-medium art, body art, etc.—are not culture-specific. Although these forms in the 1980s and 1990s conveyed a strong desire to subvert established norms in the domestic space, they did not constitute a direct counterpart of either traditional or Western art. Moreover, in the global art space, these forms provided artists from different countries and traditions with an "international language," allowing them to address both local and global issues in a highly versatile, individualized manner.

This new condition of contemporary Chinese art explains the creation of many works in this exhibition. On the one hand, these works are typical examples of contemporary art; on the other, they demonstrate the artist's effort to reengage with Chinese cultural traditions. Some of these artists have fashioned new types of book based on traditional art forms; others have derived abstract concepts from traditional book culture in making installations and multi-medium works. Far from rejecting China's cultural heritage (as critics of contemporary Chinese art customarily claim), these works indicate new ways to carry tradition into the future.

Reinventing Books

This exhibition includes four sets of "books" made separately by Lü Shengzhong, Hong Lei, Zhan Wang, and Xu Bing. Interestingly, in making these works the four artists have derived visual languages from four divergent traditions in Chinese art: folk art, urban crafts, literati aesthetics, and modern commercial art.

Among established contemporary Chinese artists, Lü Shengzhong is unique in his quest to express contemporaneity through paper-cutting— a vernacular art form associated mainly with illiterate peasant women. His first major exhibition in 1988 transformed Beijing's National Art Gallery into a solemn temple filled with totem-like images, footprints suspended in mid-air, and silhouette patterns accompanied by illegible writing. The grand spectacle of the show astonished Chinese art critics, but Lü Shengzhong sensed no victory and kept describing his art as "a lonely struggle along a desolate path."[24] In an explanation of the exhibition he wrote:

> Exerting the utmost strength, I squeeze out of a marketplace filled with contentious crowds and find a silent, forgotten little path to walk on. Intrigued by unfamiliarity and longing, I follow it to retrieve original characteristics of humankind that have been filtered out by civilization, to summon images of lost souls in the polluted air, to understand the spiritual pursuit of mankind in its infancy, and to search for the deep connections linking my native land with the rest of the world. All my effort is to nourish the empty, worn heart of modern man with the unspoiled blood of an ancient culture. Thus suddenly I gain confidence, because in my mind I have paved a spiritual path for today's art.[25]

Since then, Lü Shengzhong has continued to walk this "lonely path." The central motif of his works has remained "little red men" (*xiao hong ren*), an image transmitted by folk artists from ancient shamanism. His *Book of Humanity* in this exhibition consists of two series (pl. 31 & 32), each featuring four volumes of "red books" or "black books." He cut out red figures for the red books; the leftover scraps then became the content of the black books. The work as a whole thus embodies the most important principle of traditional Chinese cosmology—the opposition, interdependence, and transformation of *yin* and *yang*. Indeed, this principle seems to lie at the heart of paper-cutting, which always produces positive and negative forms simultaneously. Because of this significance, paper-cutting provides Lü Shengzhong with an ontological model enriched by countless metaphors: body and soul, image and text, substance and emptiness, and male and female. We can thus understand why he has titled this work *Book of Humanity*.

In contrast to Lü's rudimentary, primitive "little red men," Hong Lei's images in his three "compendia of songs" are exotic figures made of exquisite embroidery (pl. 23–29). Accompanied by embroidered lyrics, these figures represent love and desire in three masterpieces of traditional Chinese literature—*Golden Lotus*, *Dream of the Red Chamber*, and *Peony Pavilion*. According to Hong Lei, by synthesizing traditional thread-bound books, ancient painters' albums, and the art of embroidery, these compendia represent his "memory" of the literary works and his imagination stirred up by such memory. "If I have 'remade' books in any way," he says, "it is because I have interpreted the essence of these three canonical novels from a modern person's perspective.
I believe that all of man's memories are derived from texts. The desire to prolong these memories can only depend on the imagination. Thus my work serves as a type of continuation,
a dreamwalk through traditional memories."

If the thread-bound book and the painting album are conventional symbols of traditional Chinese culture, Hong Lei's use of embroidery is more closely related to his family background and personal experience. A descendant of an elite family in Changzhou, one of the old towns along the Yangzi River, he is drawn to the place's refined culture and lifestyle and has enjoyed southern music, story telling, and garden culture from childhood. In the early twentieth century, a type of embroidery was invented in the region to combine an illusionistic pictorial style imported from Europe. Hong Lei became fascinated with this type of embroidery when he worked in Changzhou's Institute of Arts and Crafts from 1989 to 1994. To him, such work testifies to the dynamic nature of Chinese art in absorbing new and foreign elements. He connects his own pursuit with this aspect of Chinese art because his goal is also to fuse ancient aesthetics and contemporary sensibility.

Since 1995, Zhan Wang has made many stainless steel rocks. By applying a pliable sheet of steel over a traditional ornamental rock and hammering it thoroughly, he could achieve a form which reproduces every minute undulation on the surface of the stone. Ranging from miniatures to monuments, his stainless steel rocks have entered various private collections and have been erected in public spaces around the world. His purpose in making these works, as he wrote in a 1996 statement, is to transform a symbol of ancient literati culture into a contemporary cosmopolitan expression:

> Placed in a traditional courtyard, rockery satisfied people's desire to return to Nature by offering them stone fragments from Nature. But huge changes in the world have made this traditional ideal increasingly out of date. I have thus used stainless-steel to duplicate and transform natural rockery into manufactured forms. The material's glittering surface, ostentatious glamour, and illusory appearance make it an ideal medium to convey new dreams [in contemporary China].[26]

Rather than satire or mockery, therefore, Zhan Wang sees his stainless steel rocks as "authentic" representations of Chinese culture in the post-modern world. The work he proposes for this exhibition continues this approach but also marks a new stage in his art: his *New "Suyuan Rock Manual"* will catalogue the stainless steel rocks he has made and sold (pl. 64). One of the most famous manuals of ornamental rocks in Chinese history, *Suyuan shipu* [Suyuan's compendium of ornamental rocks] was compiled in 1613 by the Ming dynasty scholar-collector Lin Youlin. Zhan Wang considers this type of publication a vital component of traditional rock culture. Adopting the format of *Suyuan shipu* to document his stainless rocks—recording both his motivations in making them and the histories of their collection—he is able to renew this tradition and bring it into contemporary culture.

A fourth set of "books" in this exhibition was created by Xu Bing for his *Tobacco Project*, held in 2000 at Durham in North Carolina, the center of the American tobacco industry since the nineteenth century. The main focus of the project was the relationship between James B. Duke (1865–1925)—the famed Durham tobacco tycoon—and the local economy, politics, and education. At the same time, because Duke's tobacco company was the largest cigarette producer in China in the early twentieth century, his relationship with China also inspired Xu Bing to design works for the project. This second focus is most clearly manifested in a series of "books." The centerpiece of the *Tobacco Project* was an enormous book called the *Tobacco Book* (the Chinese title is *Huangjinye shu* [Book of Golden Leaves]). Six feet wide and four feet long, it was made of dried tobacco leaves, on which Xu Bing printed a text recording the expansion of the American tobacco industry in China (pl. 60).[27] Other "books" use images of cigarette advertisements that Duke's company produced in Shanghai, the design of Chairman Mao's favorite cigarette as well as excerpts of Mao's writings, the *Dao de jing*, and Tang dynasty poems (pl. 53–59). These works are "polycentric" in both content and image: Xu Bing neither planned them as a coherent visual display nor pursued a consistent social or political theme. Instead, tobacco inspired him to create these "books" as disparate objects, each pointing to a specific memory or meditating on the implications of the cigarette to Chinese culture.

Conceptualizing the Book

Almost all examples discussed so far demonstrate a dual emphasis in the contemporary Chinese artists' engagement with the book: to abolish its literary content and to transform it into a visual, material, or aesthetic object. This emphasis also underlies the last group of works I will discuss in this introduction. Instead of taking the book as a direct subject of destruction or construction, the artists of these works distill the essential elements of traditional books and use them in conceptualizing new art projects, which may not at first glance seem related to books.

To the ancient Chinese, paper and ink—the two basic materials for printing books—were themselves aesthetic objects. Compendia have been written from the tenth century on to record and evaluate different types of paper and ink, their ingredients and methods of manufacture, formal characteristics, qualities, and histories.[28] This tradition of connoisseurship and appreciation has continued to this day.

The finest paper and ink have been named after their inventors and esteemed as works of art. Two of these inventors were Xue Tao (758?–832) and Li Tinggui (10th century). Xue Tao was a Tang courtesan famous for her beauty and literary talent. It is said that Wei Gao, the governor of Sichuan, was impressed by her poetry and recommended her for a government position of *jiaoshu*, or "collator." Although the recommendation fell through, people began to refer to her as Lady Jiaoshu. After Xue Tao accumulated sufficient resources to buy her freedom, she launched a career of paper making. Her most famous product, known as Xue Tao Paper, was valued for its extremely fine texture and delicate pink color and soon became a sought-after item by scholars and collectors.

Born into an ink maker's family in north China, Li Tinggui (whose original name was Xi Tinggui) escaped to the more peaceful South after the fall of the Tang. Learning that the Yellow Mountains was populated by thousand-year-old pine trees—the ideal material for making fine ink—he made Shezhou (later renamed Huizhou) his home. There, after repeated experiments, he finally discovered a recipe to make the best inksticks; the ingredients included pearls, drugs such as *tenghuang*, *badou*, and *xijiao*, and burned soot from the Transparent Lacquer Oil on pine trees deep in the mountains. Known as Li Tinggui Ink, the inksticks made with this recipe were fine-textured and produced subtle shades that no other ink maker had ever achieved. The emperor of the Southern Tang heard of this and requested two pieces. After painting some carps with the ink, the emperor was so pleased that he offered the humble craftsman his own surname, thus making Li Tinggui a member of the royal family. Even today, inksticks from Huizhou are still considered the best in the country.

Only by recognizing this long history of "ink and paper" culture in China can we understand the two works by Wenda Gu in this exhibition (pl. 5 & 6). Titled *Ink Alchemy* and *Tea Alchemy*, respectively, these are tokens of two much larger installations. The original installation of *Tea Alchemy* consisted of thirty thousand sheets of "green tea paper." While the method used in making the paper is traditional (Gu commissioned the best paper makers in China to produce the sheets), the material he selected—four thousand pounds of tea leaves—is unique. Slightly greenish and delicate to the point of being semi-transparent, the paper emits the fragrance of the tea. To a connoisseur of traditional arts, such paper and its products (such as the accordion-style album displayed in this exhibition) are special art objects, not merely materials for writing and painting. As art objects, they convey a particular taste associated with south China (where Gu comes from) and evoke the ancient legend of Xue Tao, who made extraordinarily fragile paper with flower petals.

The creation of *Ink Alchemy* followed the

same logic. Again, Wenda Gu commissioned the best ink factory in China to manufacture this work, but replaced the common material of pine resin or *tong* oil with a highly unconventional one—the charcoaled powder of human hair. It took Wenda Gu two years to negotiate with the factory and finally to produce the few items in this exhibition: several inksticks and test tubes containing powdered hair. Asked why he chose human hair as the material for his ink, Gu answered: "I think the hair ink is even more authentic than traditional ink because it's from Chinese people. It has Chinese DNA. In this way, I feel like it has broken past traditional ink, yet it is still deeply rooted within tradition."

Like Wenda Gu, Qin Chong also considers paper not only an art medium but also a "cultural thing":

> When I first began [making] art, I used paper for painting. But at that time, I didn't have the concept of paper that I have now. Paper is white, a blank slate; it has nothing on its surface. The process of painting on it or filling it with something is very interesting. But I think paper itself has its own meaning, too. Many developments throughout human history have been accomplished through paper. Moreover, I feel that the way that Western people and Eastern people use paper and think about paper is different. In China, for example, when someone dies, we burn paper; it's used for paper-cuts, it can be used as a window pane, we often make things out of paper, etc.—it can serve many different functions. In the West, I feel that it is more associated with printing and writing.
>
> If you use a piece of gold to make something, the material itself is very expensive. If you use a piece of paper, perhaps it doesn't have the same worth. But as an artist, I think that how you treat the material determines its role. If you bestow paper with the value and ideas that you give to gold, then perhaps that piece of paper can be a piece of gold. If you don't bestow anything on the gold, then it just remains a piece of gold.

Qin Chong's *Birthday*—a series of four paper installations in this exhibition—amply demonstrates this approach (pl. 33–36). Each installation is made of hundreds of paper sheets arranged in a neat pile. The sheets are pure white; the only image they bear is a charcoaled trace of burning. Forming a faint thread or a darkened circle, each trace has a distinctly formal characteristic and evokes a different emotional response. A Chinese viewer would immediately associate such traces of burning with the repeated destructions of books throughout China's long history, from the time of the First Qin Emperor to that of the Cultural Revolution. Qin Chong's elegant, seemingly abstract installations are therefore rich in cultural and historical meaning. They may even be considered "anti-books" because what they represent is erasure. "While books are a medium for history and memory," he reflects, "I think that this work might touch upon an opposite effect: the part that remains is blank, whereas the part that no longer exists is that which has been recorded."

Erasure is also a central element of Yang Jiecang's paintings, but it is achieved with an opposite means. To create his *100 Layers of Ink (Vast Square)*, a work in this exhibition, Yang obsessively applied layers on layers of ink, creating abstract "black holes" with shining surfaces (pl. 61). This and other works in the *100 Layers of Ink* series resulted from the artist's ambivalent relationship with traditional Chinese art and culture. On the one hand, to quote Martina Yang, Yang's painting "shows an anti-traditional, anti-cultural attitude" in eliminating images and brushwork. On the other hand, "the elimination of skill, imagery and personality is nothing less than the sublimation of the self, the ultimate aim of the cultivation of personality the Chinese literati practiced through painting and calligraphy."[29] Yang's succinct statement about the *100 Layers of Ink (Vast Square)* further reveals his intention in distilling and reusing essential elements of traditional art. As he says: "It is a conceptual work related to time, space, and the material of ink. An important factor is repetition, the aspect of multiple layers." These elements are also fundamental to the art of the traditional Chinese book.

The concept of time leads us to two other interesting works in the exhibition: Xu Bing's *Silkworm Book II* (pl. 52) and Cai Guo-Qiang's *Wako* (pl. 1 & 2). Xu's work is a sequel to his earlier *Silkworm Book,* an installation/performance project during which silkworm moths laid numerous eggs on the blank pages of a book. The eggs hatched into thousands of tiny silkworms that crawled on the pages, leaving the stained book as evidence of this biological metamorphosis. Xu Bing's current video installation restages this project. The stained book now functions as a "screen," onto which a video of the silkworms' metamorphosis is projected. In so doing, this installation restages a past performance in real time, but also translates an actual event into a visual representation.

Cai Guo-Qiang's installation in this exhibition, on the other hand, represents the concept of a large, temporal project that was never realized. Originally commissioned by the Naoshima Contemporary Art Museum in Japan, Cai conceptualized the project as a revisit to an episode in East Asian history, when *wokou,* or Japanese pirates, became a shared threat to the countries and cities in the region. According to the original plan, he was to purchase a large boat and start his journey from his hometown Quanzhou in southeast China; on board would be a rock carved with the Chinese definition of *wokou* at the time. The boat would sail to Kaohsiung, Taiwan, and then to Korea. In each place, Cai would obtain another rock, and inscribe it with the local definition of *wokou* on it. When the boat finally reached Japan, he would also inscribe the Japanese definition of *wokou* on a rock found there. In his vision, "this boat would, essentially, constitute a seafaring museum. While docking at different ports in Asia, it would collect information on *wokou* and allow an audience to view the differing histories and culture of these people."

In the end, the plan was canceled due to its possible political impact. What remains is an accordion-style album in which Cai had illustrated the project as it was originally conceived. Invented in China, this kind of portable, book-like album enables painters to make sketches and write down their thoughts on individual pages in a sequential manner. When the album is fully open, the interconnected pages also form an extended horizontal composition. Because of these characteristics, the album became especially popular among literati artists of the Ming and Qing dynasties (1368–1911), who favored an intimate mode of expression and were accustomed to writing poems alongside images. It is apparent that in making his album Cai Guo-Qiang followed this ancient tradition. It begins from Quanzhou, the starting point of the proposed journey. Images on the following pages illustrate activities at the subsequent seaports, as well as Cai's descriptions and comments. The combination of words and images, as well as the sequential reading of the album, unmistakably link the work to a traditional mode of representation.

In the installation, it is not just the album that is connected to the traditional book, however. Cai Guo-Qiang also considers the inscribed rocks a type of book: "In China, an entire mountain can be a book... For example, in Quanzhou, there is a mountain whose cliffs are inscribed with maritime stories, such as historical accounts of Zheng He's (1371–1433) travels to the Western Ocean. In this way, even nature can be considered a medium for writing books." He thus hopes "that the audience [of his installation] can understand these different types of Chinese books: the album, the rock, etc."

TO SUM UP, this introduction has demonstrated three main aspects of the close relationship between books and contemporary Chinese art. First, many book-related works in contemporary Chinese art are rooted in the artists' personal experiences. More than any other object, books awakened their curiosity about the surrounding world. The first signs of their artistic talent were often drawings in their hand-made sketchbooks. When they were growing up, diaries and other types of personal records concealed intimate memories as well as traumatic experiences during the Cultural Revolution and other political campaigns. As we have seen, such memories and experiences have motivated artists like Zhang Xiaogang, Gu Xiong, Song Dong, and Xu Bing to create deeply emotional works.

Second, to many contemporary Chinese artists, books can also be the most dangerous things in the world because they provide the most effective tools for political and religious brainwashing. Although these artists are not necessarily opposed to all books, their rebellion against orthodoxy has prompted them to cast the book as a general symbol of the repressive power of political authority. Other artists see the enormous number of books produced in the world as commercial garbage and use this phenomenon to show the decline of contemporary culture and human value. Both attitudes have led to iconoclasm or sarcasm. As attested to by many works in this exhibition, when books are taken as subjects of artistic destruction, a set of persistent strategies is invented to blaspheme and "empty" these sacred objects.

Third, because of its significance as a major transmitter of traditional knowledge, the book has become a primary site for contemporary Chinese artists to rediscover their cultural heritage and to enrich their experimental projects with their finds. Such discovery and use of tradition can be obvious or subtle. Some artists have reinvented the book as a new contemporary art genre; others have drawn inspiration from traditional books in designing installations and multi-media projects. Neither Eastern nor Western, these works derive their meaning from transgressing conventional cultural boundaries.

Rather than isolated tendencies, these three aspects are often intertwined in a single work, intensifying its complexity and historical significance. Through uncovering such complexity and significance, we hope that this exhibition can contribute to the study of contemporary Chinese art by increasing the "depth" of interpretation. This is an urgent task because now that contemporary Chinese art is becoming rapidly globalized, it is also losing its definition and individual voice. Even if works by Chinese artists are now shown in many biennales and triennials worldwide, they cannot be automatically "inserted" into the existing history of modern and international contemporary art because they are indebted to specific inspirations and conditions. By focusing on the relationship between contemporary Chinese art and the book, this exhibition explores an indigenous narrative of contemporary art in a global context, thus offering an explanation for why contemporary Chinese art is both "contemporary" and "Chinese."

NOTES

Epigraph. Philippe Vergne and Doryun Chong, ed., *House of Oracles: a Huang Yong Ping Retrospective* (Minneapolis: Walker Art Center, 2005), [pt. 2] pp. 50 & 52.

1. "读万卷书，行万里路，胸中脱去尘浊，自然丘壑内营，立成鄄鄂。随手写出，皆为山水传神矣。" Dong Qichang, *Huachanshi suibi* (China: Baoren tang edition, 1753), *juan* 2, "Hua jue," p. 1.
2. "不行万里路，不读万卷书，欲作画祖，其可得乎？" Dong Qichang, ibid., *juan* 2, p. 21.
3. Among these painters were Huang Binhong (1864–1955), Qi Baishi (1864–1957), Pan Tianshou (1897–1971), and Zhang Daqian (1899–1983).
4. Liu Haisu, "Duobian de Laimenghu [Le Lac Lema Varie]," in Shen Hu, ed., *Liu Haisu sanwen* [Three discourses on Liu Haisu] (Guangzhou: Huacheng chubanshe, 1999), pp. 76–80.
5. Yuan Hua, *Xu Beihong shengping* in Zhonghua shufa wang [Chinese Calligraphy Website], http://www.shxw.com/ReadNews.asp?NewsID=211 (accessed July 8, 2006).
6. Michael Sullivan, *The Arts of China*, 3rd ed. (Berkeley: University of California Press, 1984), p. 253.
7. This goal, first put into practice by Gao Jianfu in pursuing a new "national painting" style in the 1910s, was later summarized by Mao Zedong in the motto: *Gu wei jin yong, yang wei zhong yong*, or "Make the past serve the present; make foreign things serve China."
8. For the definition of "experimental artists," see Wu Hung, *Transience: Chinese Experimental Art at the End of the Twentieth Century* (Chicago: Smart Museum of Art, 1999), pp. 15–16.
9. The most detailed account of this art movement is provided in Gao Minglu, *Zhongguo dangdai meishu shi, 1985–86* [Contemporary art of China, 1985–86] (Shanghai: Shanghai renmin chubanshe, 1991).
10. See Gao Minglu, "Bawu meishu yundong di 'qianwei' yishi" [The 'avant-garde' consciousness in the '85 art movement], *Xiongshi meishu* no. 297 (November 1995), pp. 16–21.
11. Pablo J. Rico, "Xu Bing and the 'Well of Truth,'" in *Xu Bing: El Pozo de la Verdad* [The Well of Truth] (May–June 2004, Sala La Gallera), (Valencia, 2004), p. 268.
12. Ibid.
13. Ibid., p. 267.
14. Fei Dawei, "Two-Minute Wash Cycle: Huang Yong Ping's Chinese Period," in Philippe Vergne and Doryun Chong, eds., *House of Oracles: A Huang Yong Ping Retrospective* (Minneapolis: Walker Art Center, 2005).
15. Unless otherwise noted, all the artists' opinions herein quoted are excerpted from their full statements in this catalogue.

16. Karen Smith cited a similar statement in her *Nine Lives: The Birth of Avant-Garde Art in New China* (Zurich: Scalo, 2005), p. 335.

17. Xu Bing places extraordinary importance on the actual making of these non-sense books. See Wu Hung, "A 'Ghost Rebellion': Notes on Xu Bing's 'Nonsense Writing' and Other Works," *Public Culture* 6, no. 2 (Winter 1994), pp. 411–19.

18. Huang Yong Ping, "Yishu buxiang zhiwu" [Art—an inauspicious thing], quoted in Gao Minglu, *Zhongguo dangdai meishu shi, 1985-86*, p. 350.

19. A good introduction to Zhang Xiaogang's psychological state in that period can be found in Smith, *Nine Lives*, pp. 260–307.

20. For Zhang's debt to Surrealism and Expressionism, see ibid., pp. 266–85.

21. Li Xianting, "Wuliaogan he 'wenge' hou de disandai yishu jia" [Boredom and Third-Generation Artists in the Post-Cultural Revolution Era] (1991), quoted in Lü Peng, *Zhongguo dangdai yishushi, 1990–1999* ['90s art China] (Changsha: Hunan meishu chubanshe, 2000), pp. 95–96.

22. *China's New Art, Post-1989* (Hong Kong: Hanart T Z Gallery, 1993), p. 28.

23. Called *Reading Room*, this exhibition took place in Chambers Fine Arts Gallery in New York. For a review, see Edward Leffingwell, "Hong Hao at Chambers," *Art in America* (June–July, 2004), p. 176.

24. Lü Shengzhong, "Minjian meishu de jiben gainian" [Basic concept of folk art], *Meishu* [Fine arts], 1987, no. 10. 52.

25.Cited in Lü Peng and Yi Dan, *Zhongguo xiandai yishu shi, 1979–1989* [A History of contemporary Chinese art, 1979–1989] (Changsha: Hunan Meishu Chubanshe, 1992), p. 320.

26.Zhan Wang, "Jia shan shi" [Ornamental rock], cited in *Shoujie dangdai yishu xueshu yaoqing zhan* [The first academic exhibition of Chinese contemporary art] (Hong Kong: China Oil Painting Gallery, 1996), p. 114. A manuscript dates this writing to November 26, 1995.

27. This book no longer exists. Before the opening of the exhibition Xu Bing sprinkled it with living tobacco insects, which would gradually consume the book during the exhibition. Impossible to be collected, the book was finally destroyed by Duke University.

28. The earliest such compendium was the *Wenfang sipu* [Four compendia of objects from a scholar's studio], written by the early Song scholar Su Yijian and published in 986. Of the four compendia, two are devoted to paper and ink, respectively; the other two are about the brush and the ink stone.

29. Martina Koeppel-Yang, Introduction to Yang Jiechang's exhibition held in 2001 in the Art Museum of Hong Kong University. Manuscript provided by Koeppel-Yang to this author.

Artists' Statements & Artwork

Cai Guo-Qiang (1957–)

Born in Quanzhou, Fujian province.
1985, graduated from Shanghai Academy of Drama.
Lives and works in New York.

蔡国强

1957年生于福建泉州，1985年毕业于上海戏剧学院，现居纽约。

Wako: Japanese Pirates of the Middle Ages, 1995
Installation; stones, Chinese ink drawings on *xuanzhi* paper
Accordian-folded book: 266 x 395 cm (105 x 155½ in.)
Other dimensions variable
Collection of the artist

倭寇：中世纪的日本海盗

装置，石，水墨，宣紙

I began planning this work in 1994 in order for it to be exhibited in 1995. It was originally commissioned by the Naoshima Contemporary Art Museum, which is situated on an island off the coast of Shikoku, Japan. I wanted to produce a piece related to the history and culture of this geographic region. I chose to focus on *wokou* (J: *wako*), a term referring to Japanese pirates, because Naoshima is surrounded by numerous islands and marks one of the regions where pirates were commonly found.

Although the project was never realized, the plan was to entail the following: I would first purchase a large boat in my hometown of Quanzhou, Fujian province, measuring approximately thirty meters in length. On the boat, we would place a large rock, shaped like a Chinese bun and measuring three to four meters tall. The Chinese definition of *wokou* would be carved onto this rock. The Chinese hold a great deal of hostility towards *wokou* and view them as figures that engaged in acts of burning and pillaging.

This boat would then sail to the harbor of Kaohsiung, Taiwan. There we would acquire another rock native to the region, onto which we would carve the definition of *wokou* as it appeared in a Taiwanese dictionary. While the Taiwanese definition acknowledges the terrible deeds carried out by *wokou*, it also demonstrates a more temperate attitude by bringing to light the cultural and economic exchanges that existed between the Taiwanese and the Japanese pirates. This rock would also be placed onto the boat.

The boat would then sail to a port in Korea where we would obtain another rock. Again, the dictionary definition would be carved onto this rock, this time using Korean characters, to display the particularly hostile attitude that Koreans hold towards *wokou* as reflected in their definition of this term.

Finally, in Japan, we would also collect the Japanese definition of *wokou*. There the *wokou* are praised for their contributions to trade. During the Ming dynasty, China was locked within its own borders, refusing to engage in international trade and development. In this context, *wokou* are credited for breaking through China's trade barriers and spreading capitalist initiatives throughout the region.

Each country possesses different interpretations and evaluations of the same historical people. This boat would, essentially, constitute a seafaring museum. While docking at different ports in Asia, it would collect information on *wokou* and allow an audience to view the differing histories and culture of these people.

Ultimately, all of the carved rocks would be brought to Naoshima. The Naoshima Contemporary Art Museum is located at the top of a mountain. From the museum's entrance, we would push these rocks down the mountainside. Wherever the rocks happened to stop would be

Pl. 1. View of Cai Guo-Qiang's installation ▶
Wako: Japanese Pirates of the Middle Ages

where they would remain. The rocks' paths would be made into small trails so that visitors could follow each rock's haphazard course and read the carvings on its surface. Regardless of whether the rock ended up upright, upside-down, [or] on its side,…its final position would be permanently fixed, demonstrating the different perspectives from which history can be read and the accidental ways in which they can be formed.

In the end, this work never came to fruition. In connection with this work, I wanted to hold a scholarly symposium regarding Asian perspectives on *wokou*. As the project expanded in magnitude, the Japanese became concerned that this would cause a political incident. So the plan was canceled. What remains is an album in which I have narrated the project as it was originally conceived. I use ink brush paintings and calligraphy to tell a pictorial story. Additionally, I have small rocks, each measuring between thirty and fifty centimeters, which were collected from each country. I used calligraphy to write the dictionary definitions of *wokou* on each rock, with the text corresponding to each rock's native place. These rocks can also be considered books: each rock is an excerpt from a dictionary.

In seeing my work, I hope that the audience can understand these different types of Chinese books: the album, the rock, etc. In China, an entire mountain can be a book, a calligraphic catalogue of historical events. For example, in Quanzhou, there is a mountain whose cliffs are inscribed with maritime stories, such as historical accounts of Zheng He's travels to the Western Ocean. In this way, even nature can be considered a medium for writing books.

Based on an interview conducted by Peggy Wang in 2006.

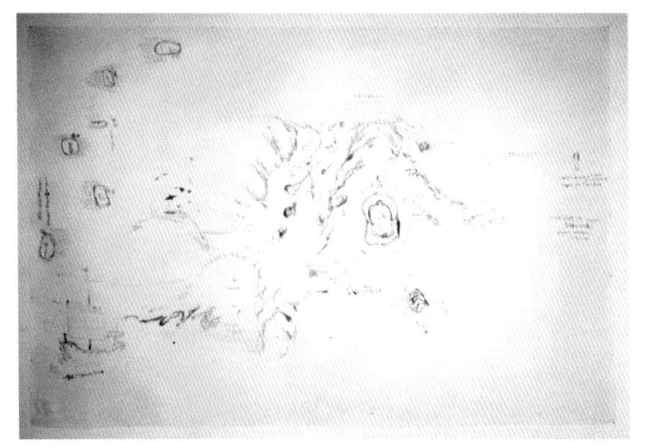

▲ Pl. 2. Leaf from accordian-folded book
Wako: Japanese Pirates of the Middle Ages

Chen Xinmao (1954–)

Born in Shanghai.
1987, received MA from Nanjing Academy of Fine Arts.
Lives and works in Shanghai.

陈心懋

1954年生于上海，1987年毕业于南京艺术学院，获得硕士学位，现居上海。

History Book Series – Blurred Printing, 2002
Xuanzhi paper, ink, mixed media
12 paintings, 48.3 x 48.3 cm (19 x 19 in.) each
Collection of Chambers Fine Art, New York

史书系列 • 错版

水墨，宣纸，综合媒材

Historical documents and images serve as the most important part of my work: they make up the work's content, structure, and visual effects. But by no means is this the case for all of my art. Since 1991 and continuing up until now, the use of books and text in some of my works, for example the *History Book* and *History Book – Blurred Printing* series, has been especially important. I am mostly interested in the origins and evolution of traditional Chinese culture and, in particular, the great disturbances and dynamic controversies of the past. In the past hundred years, pillaging and attacks have tragically destroyed our extraordinary culture, and it has hurt me a great deal.

Books and writing have had considerable influence on my work. I believe that they are an important medium for human culture. This medium can work to both connote a deeper meaning of the language (*yuyi*) as well as serve as a formal symbol (*xiangzheng*). These two qualities of "meaning" and "symbolism" are unique characteristics of Chinese art. (Other art also has them but to a different degree.) I spent ten years experimenting with these two characteristics, but learning how to employ them in an appropriate way cost me another ten years.

In 1990 I began the *History Book* series. I printed wood blocks carved with texts, such as the *Analects* and *Zizhi tongjian*, in the Song style of script. After China was liberated, there was a great deal of debate over Chinese culture. It is my belief that Chinese culture needs some kind of reinvention and reincarnation. In 1996 I began the *History Book– Ink Painting* series, in which I combined the tremendous force of ink painting with the content of historical texts and images. For this series, I combined history, archaeology, and meaningful images. I have also produced the *History Book Series–Blurred Printing*. This series is based on the concept that over thousands of years the transmission of texts has led to the deterioration of meaning. Maybe the author's original interpretation has been lost, or we've simply misunderstood it. In my works, many of the words are overlapped to the point that they cannot even be read.

Our method of reading used to be a matter of receiving information from previous generations and combining this with our current reality. Nowadays, our viewpoint is much more global: we have a broader way of viewing which didn't exist as much in the past. Traditional Chinese culture needs to be put into a broader framework and placed into a contemporary framework of time and space.

The books I've consulted are quite diverse, though mostly concerned with traditional Chinese art: calligraphy, classical books, archaeological relics, archaeological sites, etc. Recent archaeological finds as well as materials from burial culture are of particular interest to me. Traditional culture has received varying amounts of interest and interpretations throughout different historical periods. I'm most interested in the special meanings that classical texts had in

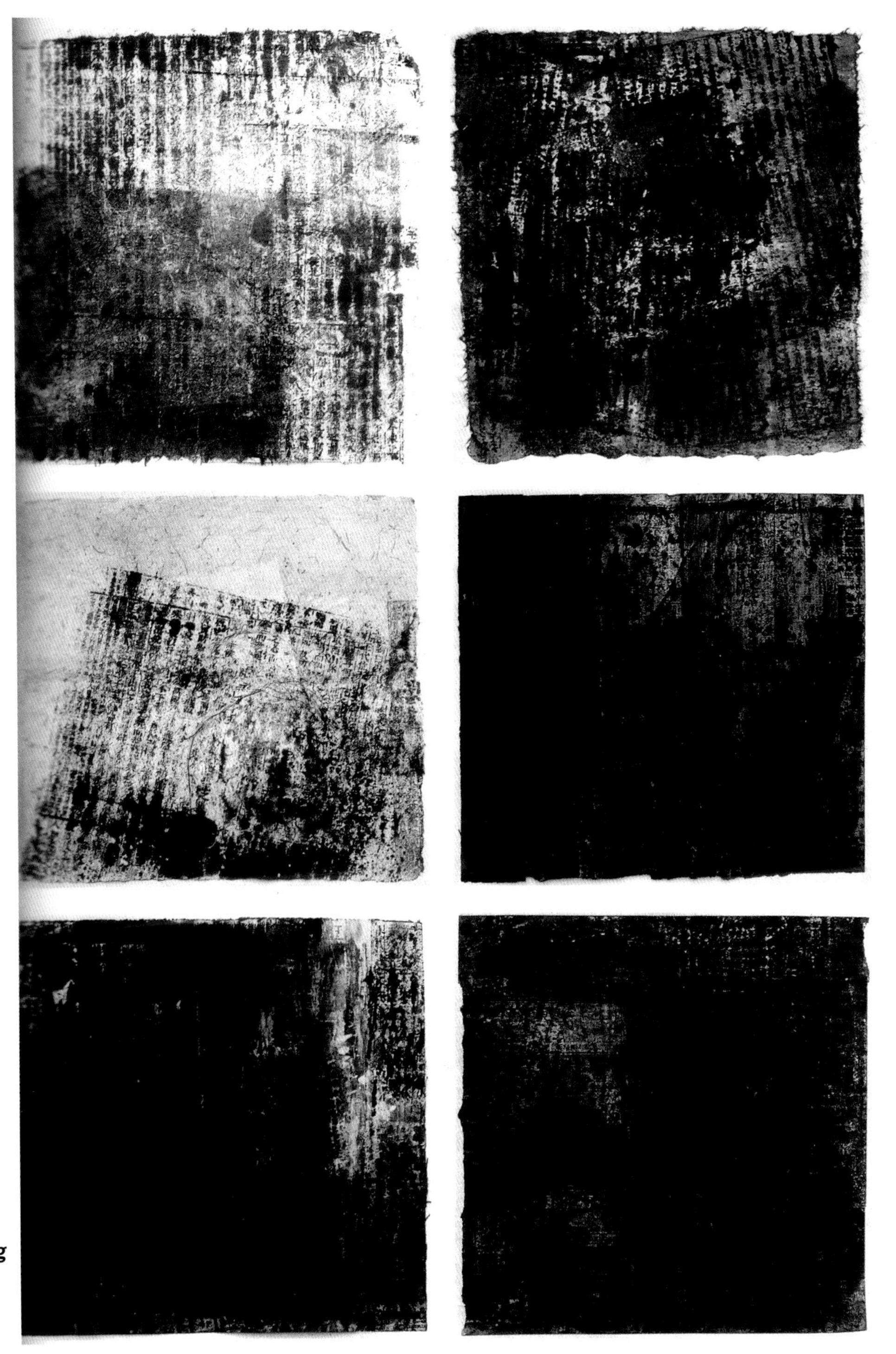

Pl. 3. Six paintings from Chen Xinmao, *History Book Series – Blurred Printing*

their contemporary times. Because I study Chinese painting, I consider ideas of history and memory in terms of traditional China. When we approach tradition, we always consider it from a modern point of view. We fix ourselves into a definitive perspective through which to interpret tradition. Secondly, we like to politicize tradition and use it for our own contemporary political purposes. There is nothing wrong with this. But we have to also consider the original meaning of traditional culture. Where is its original point of wisdom? Has it been misunderstood by us today? There is an overall breadth to traditional culture that has been neglected today. I am most interested in traditional culture's content and its original point of wisdom. I believe that the overall impact of traditional Chinese culture on today is greater than we realize. Since 1990, these ideas have been reflected in my *History Book* series.

Based on an interview conducted by Peggy Wang in 2005.

Geng Jianyi (1962–)

Born in Zhengzhou, Henan province.
1985, graduated from Zhejiang Academy of Fine Arts.
Lives and works in Hangzhou.

耿建翌

1962年生于河南省郑州市,1985年毕业于浙江中国美术学院。现居杭州。

Misprinted Books, early 1990s
18 hardcover books
27 x 19.5 x 2 cm (10⅝ x 7⅝ x ¾ in.) each book
Collection of Hanart TZ Gallery, Hong Kong

印错的书

18本精装书

I used to think that a completed artwork was like the completed act of taking a piss: when it's finished it's finished—you don't go carrying the contents of the chamber pot around with you, But now things are different, you can't just take a piss whenever you like anymore and be done with it. There are special bathrooms, like museums and art galleries, that want to expose you in your most basic acts. And doesn't everybody now accept this situation as normal? The people going in for a look are all very interested, comparing who is big and who is small. How is it that I was born in this age of organisation? [A]nd how is it that I want to be proclaimed the champ? It's really a shame.

From *China's New Art, Post-1989* (Hong Kong: Hanart TZ Gallery, 1993), p. 28.

Pl. 4. Geng Jianyi, *Misprinted Books* ▶

Each character in this series of books is formed by superimposing layers of characters. As such, these books dispel any idea of significance, and, in Johnson Chang's words, "play havoc with the traditional notion that a book is a record of valuable information." When this work was first shown in 1993, it appeared together with a group of three paintings based on images popular during the Cultural Revolution, including a giant panda inside a Red Sun – the place reserved for Mao's portrait.

Paired with this painting, Misprinted Books had a strong political implication as the artist's blasphemy of the Party's sacred doctrine. But even in that context, the work still evoked formal appreciation, as the lines after lines of misprinted characters assumed an aesthetic quality, generating a visual rhythm with a hypnotic power. Like many other works in this exhibition, therefore, Geng's books simultaneously destroy and reinvent visual forms.

—WH

Wenda Gu (Gu Wenda, 1955–)

Born in Shanghai.
1981, received MFA from Zhejiang Academy of Fine Arts.
Lives and works in New York.

谷文达

1955年生于上海,1981年毕业于浙江中国美术学院,获得美术硕士学位,现居纽约。

Ink Alchemy, 1999–2001
Installation (partial); 2 glass boxes of ink sticks made of powdered human hair, 2 wooden boxes of powdered human hair pigment, video equipment, and video film "Making Ink Alchemy"
Ink by Shanghai Cao Su Gong Ink Factory, China
Collection of the artist

墨(炼金)术

装置,人发墨,玻璃盒,木盒,影像设备,录像片
中国上海曹素功墨厂制作

Tea Alchemy, 2002
Installation (partial); 2 glass boxes of accordian-folded books made of green tea leaves, 5 stacks of tea rice paper, video equipment, and video film "Making Tea Alchemy"
Paper by Anhui Jing County Red Leaf Rice Paper Factory, China
Commissioned by the International Chado Cultural Foundation and Itoen Company, Japan, and Asia Society and Museum, USA
Collection of the artist

茶(炼金)术

装置,玻璃盒,绿茶叶纸,影像设备,录像片
中国安徽晋县红叶宣纸厂制作

Originally, these two works, *Tea Alchemy* and *Ink Alchemy*, were very large installations. For *Tea Alchemy*, I used four thousand pounds of green tea leaves in order to make thirty thousand sheets of green-tea rice paper. I call it rice paper, but it's not really rice; it just adopts the traditional method of making rice paper. But if I don't say rice paper, people won't know that it's used for painting; so I have to say "tea rice paper." In fact, "rice paper" is incorrect because it's not made from rice; it's made from straw. The formula for the ink in *Ink Alchemy* is the same as for traditional Chinese ink, only the substance is changed from charcoal powder to hair powder. I think the hair ink is even more authentic than traditional ink because it's from Chinese people. It has Chinese DNA. In this way, I feel like it has broken past traditional ink, yet it is still deeply rooted within tradition. The color is not as dark as charcoal powder because Chinese hair is not completely black.

Most of my works are produced in China; I have studios in Shanghai and Xi'an. I produce only the ink paintings here in New York. The ink paintings I do myself because I am equipped with the skills; I graduated from a Chinese ink painting department. But for the rest, I don't have the skills. How can you make paper or make powdered hair ink? I can't do it. I have to hire professional factories to do it. I don't even really convince the factories to understand my ideas. The factories where I produce my tea paper and hair ink are the most authentic places. They follow the traditional methods that have been used for hundreds of years; the rice paper factory is probably a thousand years old. I just make sure they do it properly. As an ink painter, I know which places produce the best paper and ink. Actually, among Chinese contemporary artists, only a few are graduates of Chinese painting departments. Most are from oil painting departments or sculpture departments. It [my path] is unusual because most Chinese [ink] painters just follow tradition.

On the one hand, you can use this tea paper and hair ink as materials for painting. On the other hand, you can think about what painting format can relate to DNA structures or, at least, can somehow be conceptually connected. Scientists call this the biological millennium. New genetic discoveries will change mankind in the future. It can be destructive and it can be creative. I try to link my work to this [idea] by reflecting on the cultural side of these genetic discoveries. Chinese artists have talked a lot about how to regenerate

Pl. 5. Wenda Gu, *Ink Alchemy* ▶

this scholarly treasure of ink painting for the modern era. There's always talk about this, but this is the question that my work is based on: how to create new work. Most artists, when they create a work, will change the traditional form to become something else: abstract expressionism or surrealism. It uses ink, but the format is imported from Western -isms. I don't think that this is really new. I would rather just go back to the traditional. So this is my question: how to regenerate the old tradition in order to connect to the modern era. This is why I produced new ink and new paper. Tea paper is related to Chinese tea culture, so it's still rooted to tradition. But it's brand new; it's never been done in the past. It's a kind of ecological approach. I'm still debating what kind of format would be most meaningful and appropriate for this work. The format and the meaning of the work should relate to the material itself. It should be tied together as a unit.

With the tea paper, I made Chinese accordion painting books. The accordion book can be one long horizontal scroll painting or it can be done in sections, page by page; it depends on your mood. Sometimes you create a work that can be appreciated as a single page, and when you open it, it can be a whole composition. I'm planning to do something with the tea book and hair ink together, but I'm still debating what to write or paint in the book. These are objects, but also media for the work. I'm working on a big project in Iran in April: I'm going to ship all thirty thousand sheets of green tea paper to the Iran National Contemporary Art Museum. They will select a popular local author to do a performance: the author will stay in the museum for three months and write a novel in Arabic with hair ink on the tea paper. It will be beautiful. It will also be very striking due to the political conflict in that region. This work will be a good record; it will be beautiful as a combination of different cultures.

Right now, the books are blank. The Iranian novel will be the first. Asking him to stay in the museum for three months also requires him to study the East Asian tradition—a type of meditation, an exercise of patience. If we asked him to do it in a normal environment, he would probably take longer. If I can get this done, then I will exhibit several of these books in the show. It will be a very strange thing because the paper is not really traditional rice paper, the ink is Chinese DNA ink, and it will be shown in an American institution.

Pl. 6. Wenda Gu, *Tea Alchemy* ▶

I have two possible ideas for this work: one is to exhibit the Iranian author's books; the other is to use a new book to have an interesting dialogue with the collector. What I want to do is to paint the first page of the tea book and put it on the market. When the collector wants a second piece, he can bring the book back. So that's the dialogue. Then, you can have constant talks with the collector and can educate the collector. It's not just simply that the buyer pays for and gets my object. Let's say I paint the first page, and the collector comes back wanting, for example, a second page as a gift for his wife. The relationship continues; it's more fun and more significant this way. So it's a continuation. It's like a marriage because it's an unfinished book. Usually, people present a finished book—either completely empty or completely finished, written, painted, or printed. But this process can be ongoing. Maybe we can finish the book twenty years later, and it would be totally different. Each book is a journey. [For example,] I made a book for my wife, and each year I do another painting.

People who would buy it must have an interest in this process. It's a good concept for conceptualizing the market. You can talk about the book as a commodity, but this [book] becomes a more intriguing situation because it never ends. It's fun for the collector to have a meaningful involvement. Sometimes you feel like it's too much about the commodity. My life has been involved with two periods of time: thirty years of socialism, educated with a Marxist ideology, and then twenty years of a capitalist education. The first time I opened my bank account was two years after I had lived in New York. I was scared to go to the bank; in China, I never had a bank account. I was so naïve. Sometimes, I still feel that way even though

I've been in New York for twenty years and, now that the market is so hot, anything that I paint will be gone. The buyers are just waiting. In China, I used to create art as something against government rule. Here I paint things as commodities. Sometimes, I feel disgusted. It's a psychological thing that goes back and forth. This work would also be a result of creating something that is more fun; at least, the collector will have more of a dialogue with me.

You can do this with the audience, too. This would result in a more interesting aspect for the show. Usually, the show gathers comments from the public. My installation could be set up to take their comments. When it's finished, it could be very beautiful: different styles, colors... This is not an involvement with the collector, but rather an involvement with the institution and public. So it's a kind of interactive and participatory work. I'm still trying to think which kind is best, and I will decide right before the show. If I do it with the audience, I always think about convenience. The comments are more important than the materials themselves. So they can use normal pens or a brush or whatever. That would be a very interesting process. And in the China Institute, at least, the people would be specifically interested in Chinese culture.

This work will display a tea accordion book, a few ink sticks, and powdered hair in test tubes (from the lab as a symbol of genetic ink). It looks very simple, but each part took me two years to negotiate with the factory and to finally produce the results. The whole installation will be designed as an aesthetic experience. I will consider the audience's thoughts when viewing this show: what are their expectations from Chinese culture? what is their involvement with Chinese culture? what should the China Institute be? In this way, I'm not just displaying the final result like a silent object.

Based on an interview conducted by Peggy Wang in 2005.

Gu Xiong (1953–)

Born in Chongqing, Sichuan province.
1985, received MFA from Sichuan Fine Arts Institute.
Lives and works in Vancouver, British Columbia.

顾雄

1953年生于重庆，1985年毕业于四川美术学院，获得美术硕士学位，现居加拿大温哥华。

Cultural Revolution Sketch Books, 1972–76
Ink and pencil on paper
10 original sketch books and 10 replicas:
22.9 x 22.9 x 5.1 cm (9 x 9 x 2 in) each
Collection of the artist

文化大革命速写本
墨，铅笔，纸

For this exhibition, I'm displaying a set of sketchbooks from my youth during the Cultural Revolution. At sixteen, I was sent to the countryside to be "re-educated." I spent four years in the countryside of Dabashan in Sichuan, an impoverished area located on the border between Sichuan and Shaanxi province. We couldn't predict what lay ahead and couldn't see our own futures. In those conditions, I started to use sketchbooks to record my life. I bound most of the sketchbooks myself with a needle and paper.

I went from the excitement of the Cultural Revolution to the remote countryside and began to reflect on the conditions of the revolution. Despondency about the realities of my life and the unpredictability of the future lingered and wandered back and forth in my mind. These all compelled me to draw. Every morning, I would carry my sketchbooks with me. When we took a break from physical labor, I would pull them out and draw images of the peasants or the scenery. At night, I would sit under a kerosene lamp and recollect my experiences from the day. I would find what was meaningful from that day and draw it. In those four years, I produced about twenty or so sketchbooks.

I ended up leaving those sketchbooks at my mother's house, and in 1989 I left China for Canada. In 1998 I returned for the first time, at which point I found these sketchbooks at my mother's house and brought them back with me. In 2002, the Belkin Art Gallery of the University of British Columbia organized an exhibition of art from the Cultural Revolution, which included propaganda art and posters from private collections in China. The curator saw my sketchbooks and became extremely interested in them because, at that point, all of the works in the exhibition were propaganda pieces. My sketchbooks revealed an individual person's reflections, experiences, and internal thoughts during that period of time. They thought that the private feelings expressed in the sketchbooks would produce a meaningful dialogue with the fanaticism present in the political propaganda.

I've been thinking about another project in which I would connect the experiences I had before and after immigrating to Canada. If one thinks of the Cultural Revolution as a political movement, then we were victims of this movement. Since 1989, I have chosen and followed my own path: that is, coming to the West to practice contemporary art and to lead a new life. In the past sixteen years, the hardships I have endured here far exceeded the ones I experienced during the Cultural Revolution. To come to a new country with no language, cultural understanding, and social background, you are essentially deaf and mute. The experiences I had when first coming here are similar to ones during the Cultural Revolution. Given this, we can think about how one goes from the Cultural Revolution to a personal cultural revolution and how the two can be contrasted.

I think this experience [passage from one revolution to another] is significant because it began with a background set under the conditions of globalization. Globalization is not something just from the past ten years. The utopian thinking of the Cultural Revolution and Communism can also be considered a form of globalization. This is

◀ **Pl. 7. "Paean to Life." Illustration from Gu Xiong, *Cultural Revolution Sketchbooks***

▼ **Pl. 8. Five of Gu Xiong's *Cultural Revolution Sketchbooks***

not to say whether globalization is good or bad. To me, this is not important. What's important is that within different cultural experiences, we can seek our own personal space. Whether today or during the Cultural Revolution, globalization has provided us with the possibility for this. During the Cultural Revolution, of course, we could only do this in secret. But today in the West, within this age of cultural exchange and cultural blending, everyone has the possibility to find his own space. Regardless of whether you're in your own country or if you've immigrated to a new place, you will be confronted and challenged by other cultures. This will force you to rethink the cultural environment and space in which you live. In the present age, with the Internet, you can find out anything about any corner of the world. What's important is that we don't just stand idle in this context, but rather consider how to study other cultures and ways of thinking and synthesize them to broaden our current cultural space.

At the time that I made these sketchbooks, they were a way of recording reality. I think that the book, particularly if you make it yourself,

◀ **Pl. 9. "Welcoming the sunrise." Illustration from Gu Xiong, *Cultural Revolution Sketchbooks***

▼ **Pl. 10. "Xiaowei and I grinding wheat at midnight." Illustration from Gu Xiong, *Cultural Revolution Sketchbooks***

is an extremely individual and unique format. When this personal format reaches the public, even if the audience has had different experiences, it will still resonate with them.

When you touch a book, you can really feel that it has existed in history, in a cultural space. You can pick it up and take part in some of its temporal and spatial experiences. Even if I make a new

Pl. 11. "Breaking rocks for materials." Illustration from Gu Xiong, *Cultural Revolution Sketchbooks*

copy of a sketchbook for viewers to touch, it will itself become a meaningful work. It will no longer be a piece just for me, but will be something used and read by a broader public. When it returns to me, it will have been transformed.

If I were to remake this work today and include my present experiences, I might change it into a handscroll format. Visually, the handscroll can incorporate both text and movement. Moreover, it can be viewed very intimately, bit by bit, or can be exhibited as a continuous whole. This would maintain both a sense of the traditional as well as sustain a feeling of contemporary visual culture.

Another format that I have considered is an audiobook, which would incorporate both music and sound. While the viewer is flipping through a sketchbook or looking at a handscroll, he would also be able to listen to an audio component. This could include recordings, songs, discussions, etc. documented from the Cultural Revolution. What I find very peculiar is that my experiences, visual imagination, and memories in China before 1989—from my youth and through the 1970s and 1980s—can all be aroused through a song.

Pl. 12. "So hard to walk on the road!" Illustration from Gu Xiong, *Cultural Revolution Sketchbooks*

Pl. 13. "The first study meeting in eight months." Illustration from Gu Xiong, *Cultural Revolution Sketchbooks*

Pl. 14. "Very educational." Illustration from Gu Xiong, *Cultural Revolution Sketchbooks*

But after immigrating to Canada in 1989, the audio was replaced by the visual. In a new environment and slightly older, one finds that reality must be confronted on a daily basis, and there is no interest in learning a new song. I am very interested in these differences between visual memory and audio memory.

Based on an interview conducted by Peggy Wang in 2005.

Pl. 15. "Our compound."
Illustration from Gu Xiong,
Cultural Revolution Sketchbooks

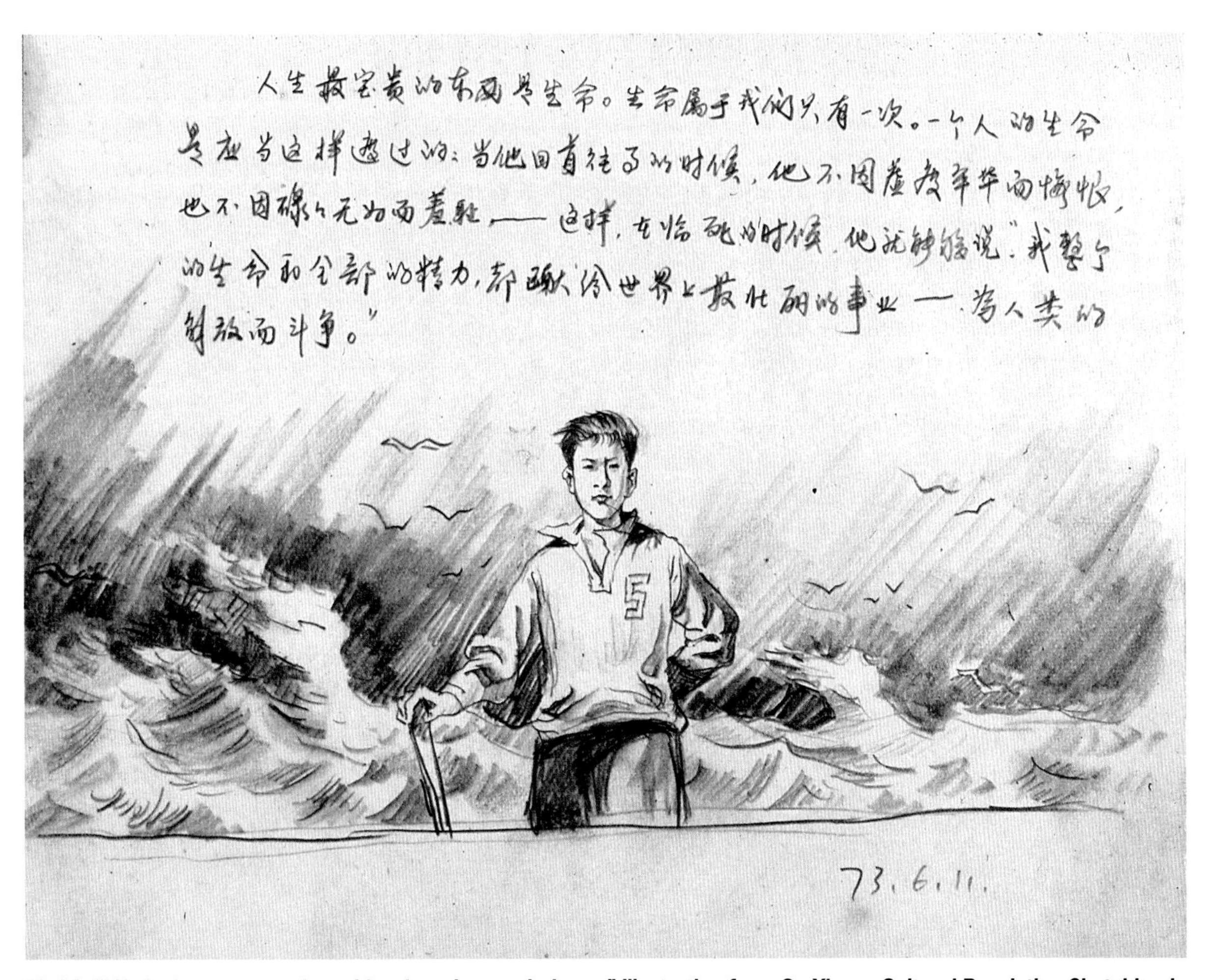

Pl. 16. "Life is the most precious thing for a human being...." Illustration from Gu Xiong, *Cultural Revolution Sketchbooks*

Hong Hao (1965–)

Born in Beijing.
1989, graduated from Central Academy of Fine Arts.
Lives and works in Beijing.

洪浩

1965年生于北京，1989年毕业于中央美术学院，现居北京。

Mexico-Huun-Amate, 2004
Installation; paint on Hahnemühle paper, plexiglass case
40 x 62.2 x 3.8 cm (15¾ x 24½ x 1½ in.)
Collection of Chambers Fine Art, New York

墨西哥-昏-阿玛泰

装置，纸，有机玻璃

Selected Scriptures II, 1994–2000
Accordion-folded book illustrated with fifteen screenprints
Each page: 36.5 x 26.4 cm (14⅜ x 10⅜ in.)
Collection of the Museum of Modern Art, New York

藏经

丝网印

The History of Modern Art, 2004
Two vintage copies of H. H. Arnason, *The History of Modern Art* (Chinese edition: 1983; English edition: 1978)
29.2 x 73 x 28.6 cm (11½ x 28¾ x 11¼ in.)
Collection of Chambers Fine Art, New York

西方现代美术史

旧书

Since 1988, I have produced works related to books and printing. When I first started, I was a student in the Printmaking Department at the Central Academy of Fine Arts. In the Printmaking Department, we learned all aspects of printing. Because both printmaking and printing books share this process of "printing," I began to produce prints of books. I used silk-screening to print an image of an open-faced book on a sheet of paper. Its dimensions and details lend it the appearance of an extant book. If you didn't see the original work, you would think that this was a real book. But in reality, it's just a printed image of a book on a flat surface.

At the time, the production of books was very much related to my understanding of art. In the 1980s it was difficult to see contemporary art or Western art exhibitions, so we learned about contemporary art through catalogues. These catalogues let us access and understand the origins and conditions of contemporary art. At the same time, these catalogues seemed to symbolize a level of achievement. Of course, as students, we couldn't have catalogues of our own works. If your work appeared on even one page, that was considered impressive. But that almost never happened. So I printed an image of a catalogue and featured my own work inside. The catalogue adopts the appearance an old book, although the content is contemporary. I experimented also with Western-style catalogues and different book formats.

After 1992, I produced a series of prints that looked as if they were all collected from one book. I kept the binding and text along the fore-edge of the book consistent to indicate that they were all pages from the same source. Moreover, all of the prints have different page numbers. In fact, I followed the order and format of a real book [, in which] the first page of the book is the preface. In the "preface," however, I've included advertisements and fabricated sponsors and awards. The content of the entire book is also varied: it includes text, maps, traditional-style paintings, and pictures. The maps I've included have been re-arranged so that the sizes, positions, names, topography, etc. of the countries are not what one would expect. For example, on one map, the size of each country is correlated to its political power. In the "postscript," I've mixed the Chinese

Pl. 17. Hong Hao, *Mexico-Huun-Amate*

and English together so that it's illegible. In fact, the entire book cannot be read.

We use books for specific purposes. When we go to the library or bookstore, we look for books that we need. If you're looking to learn a foreign language, you will buy a foreign language textbook. Here, however, I have taken away the functionality and contextual continuity of the book. Although all of these pages are supposedly from one book, you don't actually know what this book is about. In real books, the first page is related to the second page, etc. In my book, however, the contents of each page are independent of each other. I've revised the structure so there is no longer a sense of continuity. Although I've used the format of the book, I've taken away what one thinks a book should be. This book can't be used to find answers. This same principle applies to the maps: the longer you use them, the more confused you will become. I spent about twelve years, from 1988 to 2000, on prints from this book.

Last year, I had a solo exhibition called "Reading Room" at Chamber's Fine Art in New York. All the works had to do with reading and books. For example, in my work *AiA*, I reversed the process for producing a book. Books usually start with a draft and then reach a final product. In *AiA*, however, I've started from the final product. I traced the entire surface of an issue of *Art in America*, copied all the text, and left the illustrations blank. Again, I've removed its functionality so that only the shape and form remain.

A work I'm exhibiting in this show, *Mexico-Huun-Amate*, is also a book without content. This book is also completely devoid of text. Instead, there is only paper onto which I've used a brush to paint fibers to give the appearance of handmade paper. The absence of the book's content leaves the viewer only to read the fibers of the page.

In another work, I bought several hundred books, and from each book, I removed a portion to be bound in an entirely new book. I then put my name and an image of my own work on the front cover to resemble a biennale catalogue. It's possible to imagine that the images in this catalogue are of pieces exhibited in a biennale.

Pl. 18. Two-page spread from Hong Hao, *Selected Scriptures II*

Selected Scriptures is a large collection of silkscreen prints, which took the artist several years to realize. In a sophisticated illusionistic style, each print represents a picture in an imaginary encyclopedia; the page number indicates its position in the book. The encyclopedia, however, is never realized in the material form of a book. The diverse subjects of the prints, the random use of multiple languages, and the heterogeneous origins of pictorial motifs further defy any rational structure and coherent layout.

—WH

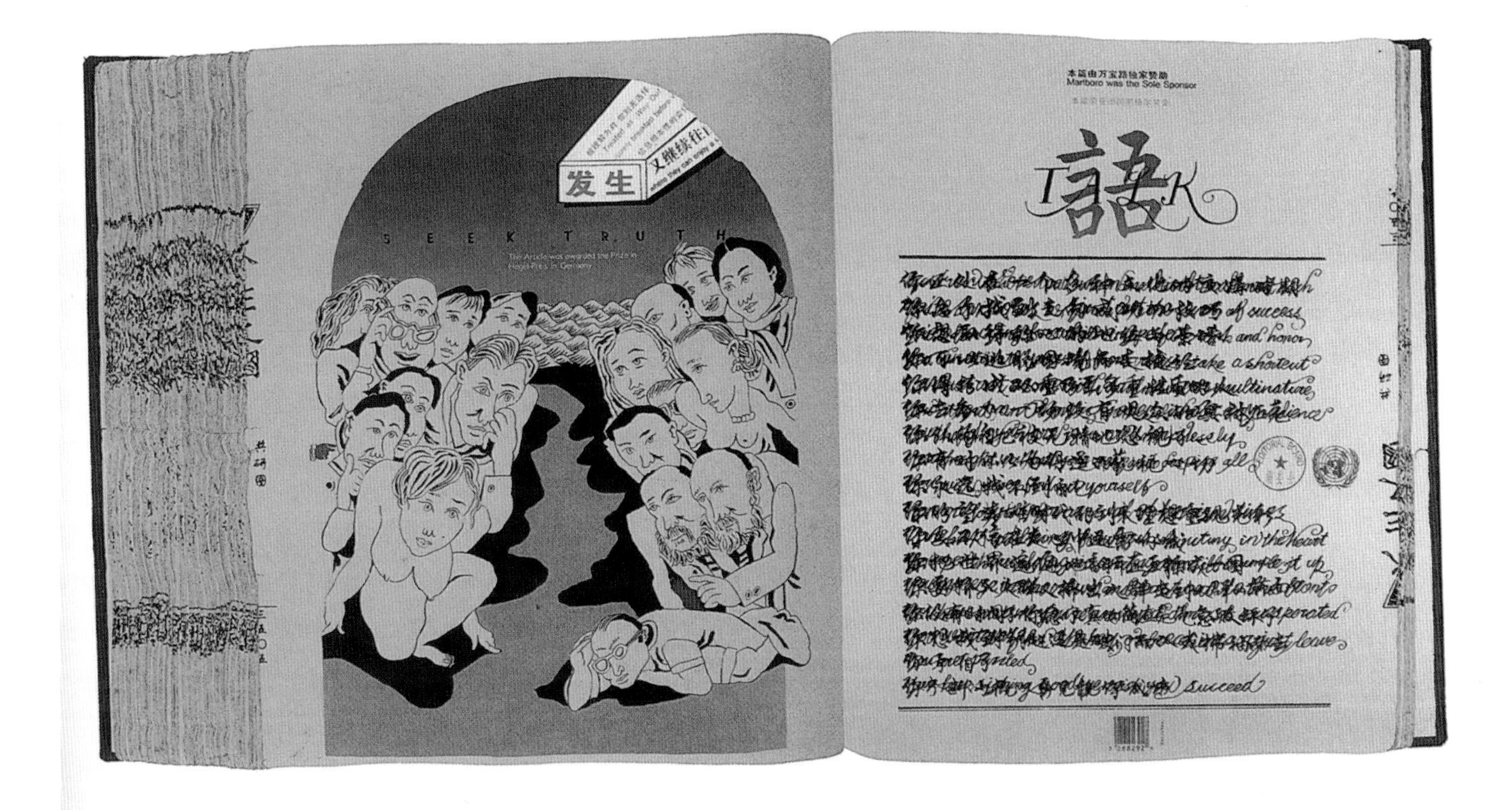

Pl. 19. Two-page spread from Hong Hao, *Selected Scriptures II*

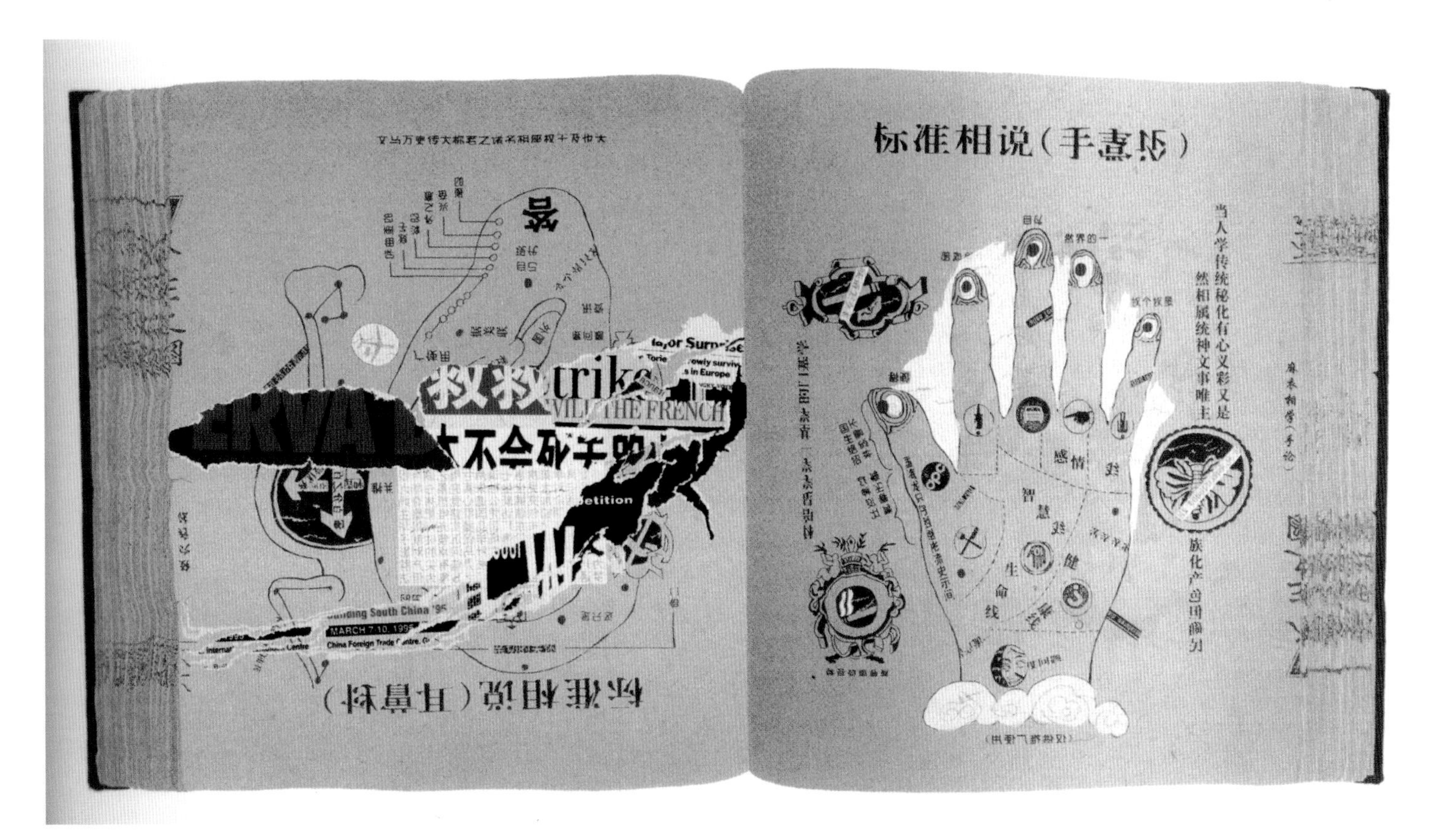

Pl. 20. Two-page spread from Hong Hao, *Selected Scriptures II*

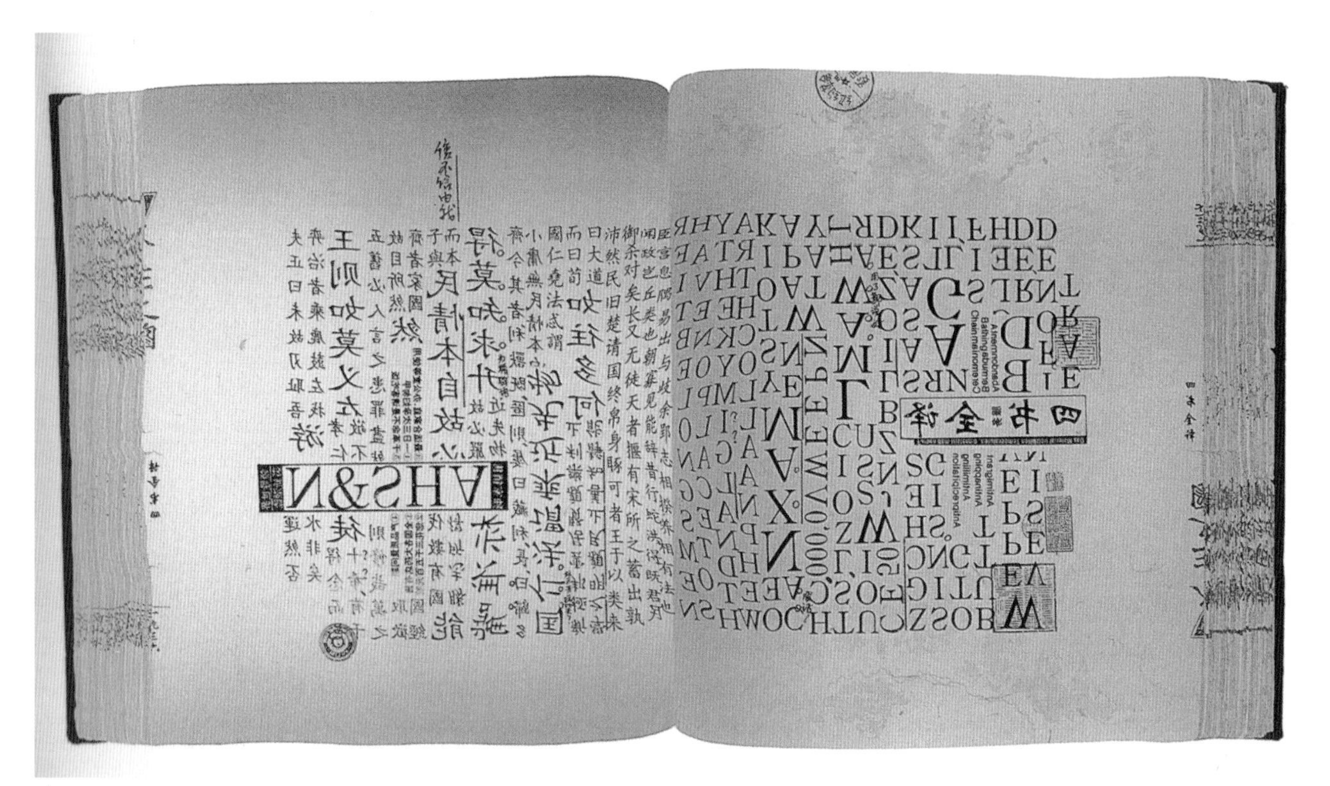

▲ Pl. 21. Two-page spread from Hong Hao, *Selected Scriptures II*

Its ordering and format still adhere to a real book, including a page of introduction and acknowledgments. When I arrange the content of these books, I still try to maintain a visual connection between opposing pages. Although the pages are drawn from different sources, it appears as though there could be a possible relationship between the two, but you can't say for certain what it is. Some of the images are scanned in, but some are ripped directly from the original texts. It's not a matter of destroying books, but a matter of repositioning them into new ones. My interest is in the origins and narrative of the catalogue. After a book has been published, it organizes an economic reality and tries to show people how something *should* be. Catalogues abide by certain standards and rules, but mine defy the function, structure, and production expected of books.

Based on an interview conducted by Peggy Wang in 2005.

▼ **Pl. 22. Hong Hao, *The History of Modern Art***

Hong Lei (1960–)

Born in Changzhou, Jiangsu province.
1987, graduated from Nanjing Academy of Art.
Lives and works in Changzhou.

洪磊

1960年生于江苏常州，1987年毕业于南京艺术学院，现居常州。

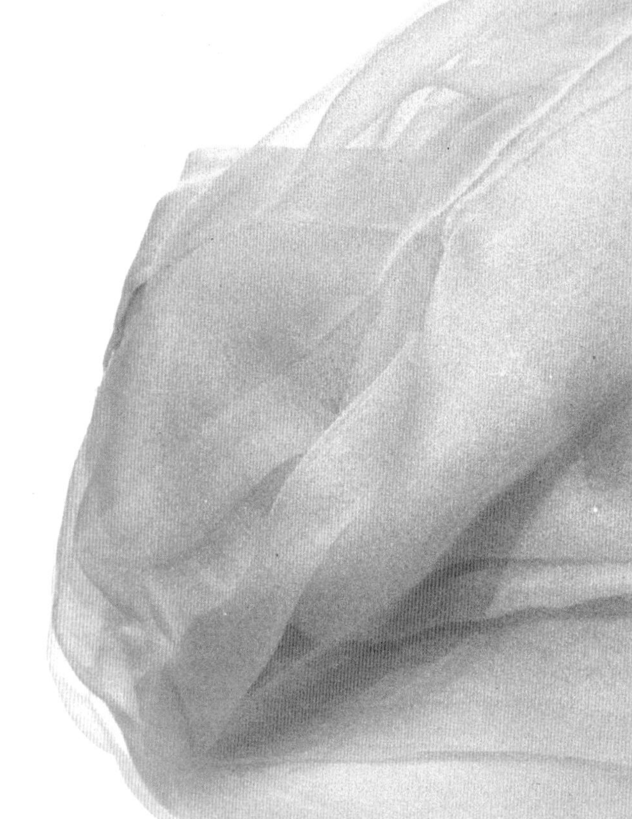

Three Compendia of Songs, 2006
Books made of embroidery; silk
25 x 15 cm (9⅞ x 6 in.) each
Collection of the artist

(1) *Compendium of Songs from Dream of the Red Chamber*
(2) *Compendium of Songs from The Golden Lotus*
(3) *Compendium of Songs from The Peony Pavilion*

三种曲谱
丝绸，刺绣

(1) 红搂梦词曲谱
(2) 金瓶梅曲谱
(3) 牡丹亭曲谱

My works in the exhibition use the book as their medium. In traditional China, pieces of embroidery have often been exhibited independently of each other. Although my *Compendium of Songs from the Golden Lotus*, *Compendium of Songs from Dream of the Red Chamber*, and *Compendium of Songs from the Peony Pavilion* all lack a narrative structure, they are nevertheless bound together as an indivisible whole. In Chinese, *pu*, or "compendium," is defined as "a catalogue that categorizes and systematizes things." In my three compendia, I employ love and desire as an organizational principle. Thus it was only natural for me to use books. My interest is actually in embroidery, but the format and method of the traditional Chinese book or album add to its mystery.

Books are something I've revered since I was a child. I've always wanted to produce a book, and I've had this inspiration, perhaps subconsciously, for thirty years or so. "Books" in traditional China have been regarded as sacred objects, a concept arising from Confucianism. From Qin and Han dynasty bamboo strips to later thread-bound books, they all capture the pious devotion of generations of Chinese people. In this way, the production of my "book" is both a Confucian rite and a mysterious journey home.

I am interested in traditional thread-bound

books, ancient painters' albums, and the mounting of folk embroidery from the Jiangnan region. If I have "remade" books in any way, it is because I have interpreted the essence of these three canonical novels from a modern person's perspective. I believe that all of man's memories are derived from texts. The desire to prolong these memories can only depend on the imagination. Thus my work serves as a type of continuation, a dreamwalk through traditional memories.

Based on an e-mail interview conducted by Peggy Wang in 2005.

▲ **Pl. 24. Hong Lei, *Compendium of Songs from Dream of the Red Chamber***

◀ **Pl. 23. Two leaves from Hong Lei, *Compendium of Songs from Dream of the Red Chamber***

▲ Pl. 25. Hong Lei, *Compendium of Songs from The Golden Lotus*

Pl. 27. Two leaves from Hong Lei, *Compendium of Songs from The Golden Lotus* ▶

▲ Pl. 26. Hong Lei, *Compendium of Songs from The Golden Lotus*

初相會可意人年少青春不上二旬黑鬖
鬖鬖兩朶烏雲紅馥馥一點朱唇臉夭
桃手如嫩笋若生在畫閣蘭堂端的也
有個夫兮可惜在章臺出落做下品但
能够改嫁從良勝強似棄舊迎新

Pl. 28. Two leaves from Hong Lei, *Compendium of Songs from The Peony Pavilion*

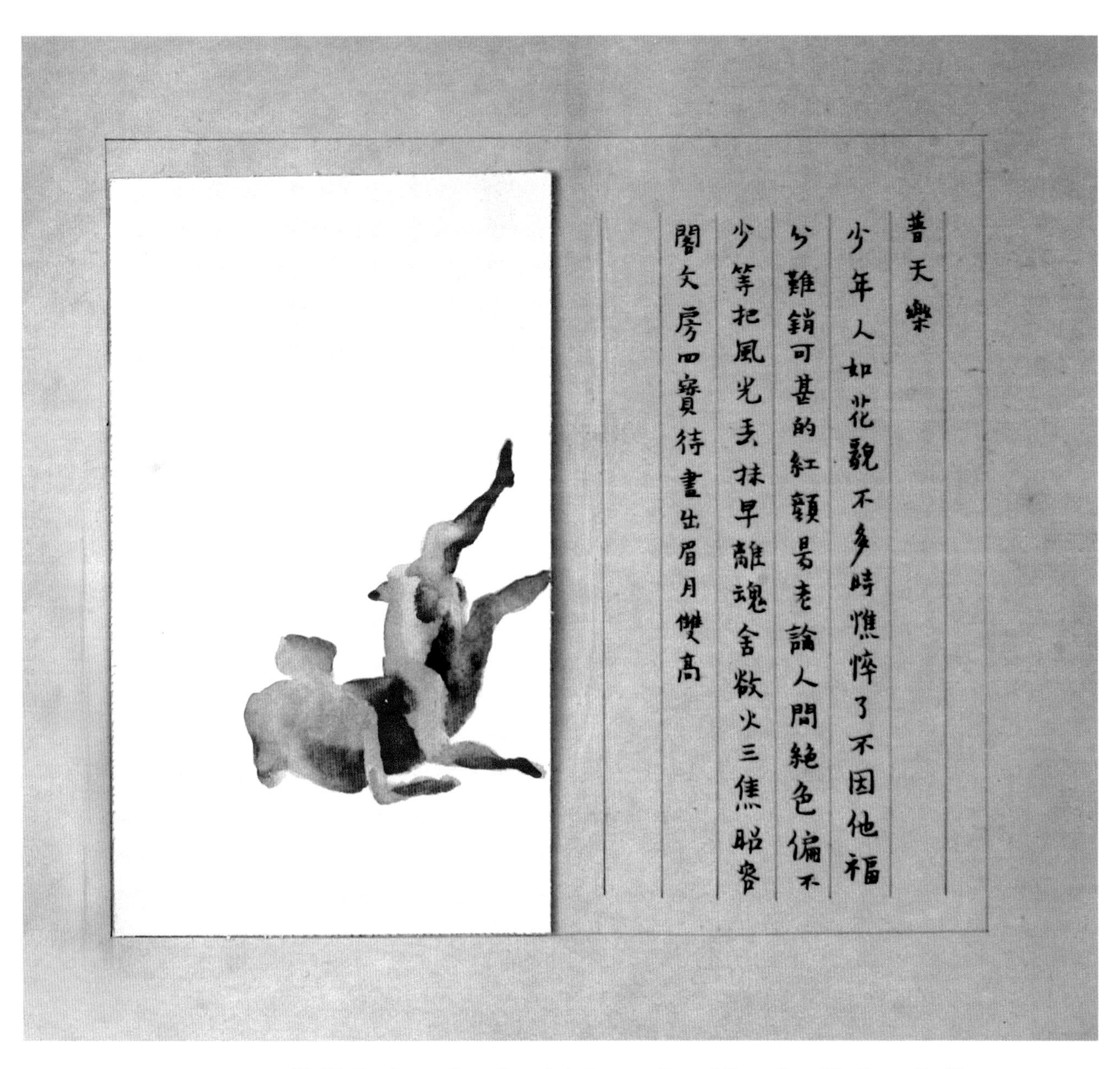

Pl. 29. Two leaves from Hong Lei, *Compendium of Songs from The Peony Pavilion*

Liu Dan (1953–)

Born in Nanjing. 1981, graduated from Jiangsu Chinese Painting Academy. Lives and works in New York.

刘丹

1953年生于南京，1981年毕业于江苏省国画院，现居纽约。

Dictionary, 1991
Watercolor on paper
213 x 304 cm (7 x 10 ft.)
Collection of HSBC Bank, N.A.

民国小字典
纸本水彩

The micro-cosmos is something which can be made perceptible by a viewer's becoming engrossed in matter...In overcoming one's fear of death one inevitably discovers unknown and essential aspects of the self. This is also why painting is seldom a pleasure to me. More often I am in a state of sadness and ecstasy.

From an interview between the artist and Xu Lei, as cited by Alice Grünfelder, "Modern Painter in Brush and Ink," http://www.culturebase.net/print_artist.php?3317 (accessed June 14, 2006).

Those of my generation in China were born sick, with a mental disease. It was truth versus life: If you cheat, you live; if you defend the truth, you die. Our psychological damage is a deep darkness, something you can't see through. Some use their scars to become heroes, others give up hope altogether, and a few try to get better, to understand. One reason I have chosen to paint with brush and ink is because my touch cannot lie to the paper. Each stroke is my record. In healing, the most important element is patience...Perhaps that is why I paint the way I do.

From *Alternative Visions: Hiromitsu Morimoto & Liu Dan* (New York: Takashimaya Co. Ltd, 1993), p. 9.

Like the natural world, a dictionary offers raw materials—words and definitions, not digested discourses and narratives. Reading a dictionary resembles exploiting a mine or excavating an archaeological site, activities which evoke the feeling of making original discoveries and discovering one's roots. The dictionary also arguably has the longest shelf life of any book, as one can never finish "reading" it but will endlessly return to it for help.

This impressive painting captures these sensibilities. By magnifying an ordinary dictionary hundreds of times its original size, the artist bestows on it the status of a monument. By depicting the dictionary with a painstaking, photorealistic style, he stresses its vulnerability to time and to human touch: the book's yellowish paper and worn pages arouse nostalgia, testifying to an intimate relationship with a human subject.

—WH

Pl. 30. Liu Dan, *Dictionary*

Lü Shengzhong (1952–)

Born in Dayuji village, Shandong province.
1978, graduated from Shandong Normal University; 1987, received MA from Central Academy of Fine Arts.
Lives and works in Beijing.

吕胜中

1952年生于山东省平度县大鱼脊山村，
1978年毕业于山东师范大学，1987年毕业
于中央美术学院，获得文学硕士学位，现居北京。

The Book of Humanity, 2002–2004
Set of 8 books (4 red and 4 black); paper, fabric, silk thread
Each book: 43.8 x 33.7 x 1.27 cm (17¼ x 13¼ x ½ in.)
Collection of Chambers Fine Art, New York

人文书

剪纸，线装本

I don't start out by intentionally using books in my art. In art, I think of the book as a form or shape. It's a medium for communicating with people, and in this way it isn't much different from art itself. I think that the creation of an artwork doesn't first originate with the medium or choice of material, but rather comes about from an idea. One only uses a book when it is most appropriate to conveying the idea.

In 2003, for the Venice Biennale, I exhibited a work entitled *Landscape Study*. For this work I built a study, a room full of books. This wasn't a matter of making a book, but rather making a work out of books. In this room, the book served as a building material and was used to reflect a certain world view. I used Chinese landscape to express a traditional world view and connected this concept of "Chinese landscape" to books with various types of content. I went to publishing companies, to bookstores, [and] to antique markets, and bought six thousand books. They dealt with different subjects ranging from classical to modern and were written in Chinese or English. I replaced all of the book jackets and used the spines as a canvas to paint a section of Dong Yuan's *Scenery Along the Xiao and Xiang Rivers*. When all the books were lined up on the shelf, they formed one section of the handscroll. Even though the contents of the books varied greatly, they all became encompassed within this larger concept of "Chinese landscape." For example, a philosophical text might appear very serious. But when the original book jacket is replaced with a Chinese landscape painting, the viewer's reaction towards it changes too. Yet, upon opening the book, the content is still the same.

For the work *Book of Humanity*, I make my own books. When I exhibited *Book of Humanity* at Chambers Fine Arts last year, for example, I made a whole new set of books composed of Chinese cutouts and divided the volumes into red books and black books. I cut out red figures for the red books, and the leftover scraps became the content of the black books. I made ten volumes, all different. The layout of the figures in the book was arbitrary, based freely on a feeling, based on an idea, based on an imagined story...This is a case of starting from no book to creating a new book.

Renwen shu, or *The Book of Humanity*, is the story of man. Chinese is a pictorial language, so its writing refers both to text and pictures. In Chinese, the title of this book indicates that it takes one man (*ren*) as a Chinese character (*wenzi*). However, translating this meaning into English is a bit complicated. *Renwen* (humanity) as a phrase suggests *renlei* (humankind) and *wenming* (civilization) as well as *wenhua* (culture). However, as single characters combined together, *ren* and *wen* can also refer to man's language. Rather than giving these characters or phrases specific

▲ **Pl. 31. Black books from Lü Shengzhong, *The Book of Humanity***

meanings, I feel that it is better to think of this as a book about life. This book doesn't use modern writing to tell a story, but rather uses the cutout of a man's form. This man's form, the Little Red Figure, can take four directional positions. Including both the front and back sides, there are a total of eight symbols available. This is similar to the "Eight Character Incantation" in Buddhism. With eight, you can make a universe. With eight, you have enough. Different arrangements can make up different stories or landscapes of humanity, and these arrangements will never repeat. I don't try to distinguish between the front and the back of the figure. The fact is that there are two sides to everything. You can't say that one side is important and one side is unimportant.

Although the book doesn't have any words inside, a reader is able to flip through it page by page all the same. Can the books be read? Certainly, the books hold the possibility for being read. The question is only how one interprets the concept of "reading."

There is both a traditional Chinese bound version of the book and a Western hardcover version. I arranged the contents of each page on the computer, some vertically and some horizontally. The Western bound book is horizontally arranged, while the Chinese bound book is vertically arranged. If a Westerner sees the traditionally bound Chinese book, he may already have the preconceived idea that it is a piece of art and cannot be read. A Chinese viewer, on the other hand, is already familiar with this type of book and so will assume its contents to be legible. If a Westerner sees the Western bound book, he will immediately recognize it as a book. I think his reaction to this book and to the traditional Chinese bound book will be different. It depends on his expectations according to the book's initial appearance. In short, these works are not just for Chinese viewers. We are not trying to create a traditional or conventionally readable book. It is an art book. The book's contents and concept are, in reality, very different from the normal books that publishing companies produce. But I personally think that the exterior needs to appear even *more like a book than a book.* They look more real than real books.

Based on an interview conducted by Peggy Wang in 2005.

▼ **Pl. 32. Red books from Lü Shengzhong, *The Book of Humanity***

Qin Chong (1968–)

Born in Xinjiang.
1990, graduated from Beijing Art and Design College.
Lives and works in Guangzhou and Berlin.

秦冲

1968年生于新疆,1990年毕业于北京工艺美术学校,现居广州与柏林。

Birthday I, II, III, IV, 2002
Installation of 4 units; paper, wood
80 x 80 x 97 cm (31½ x 31½ x 38¼ in.) each
Collection of the artist

生日I, II, III, IV
装置, 纸, 木

When I made this work, *Birthday*, I didn't think specifically about books, but I like the idea of it being included in this exhibition. In truth, every work is a book. But the way in which each is written varies a great deal. The way that I've written my "books" is through writing without words. Books use words for recording history. Yet, my works use a different form for documentation and elicit a new method for reading. Audience members who stand in front of my works feel that there is content there, even if it's not explicitly written out. Perhaps this is a special characteristic of contemporary art: it's not limited to any form. In my piece, the parts that have been burnt are similar to written records in that they both evidence something that has already taken place. And yet, the part that we see hasn't been written on at all. I feel that these two parts form a very poignant dialogue, particularly arranged in such a neat and tidy way. Thus while books are a medium for history and memory, I think that this work might touch upon an opposite effect: the part that remains is blank, whereas the part that no longer exists is that which has been recorded. As such, the audience thinks more about that which is absent. People often feel that paper should be used for recording something. However, I have used the paper not merely to record something, but to make an artwork. The choice of material and what one personally wants to express are closely related. A lot of artists choose new materials as a way of completing the medium. But I feel that materials should be used to complete one's ideas. I have other works that have to do with books, too, although my considerations are perhaps more in traditional Chinese art, and my choice of medium is usually that which is most appropriate to the ideas.

There is another part to my work that is also very difficult to explain. Whether the works are exhibited in Europe or China, audience members all seem to experience a similar feeling: they tell me that they can detect a very strong sense of an Eastern culture or spirit. But at the same time it looks entirely new, and there are no explicit Chinese symbols present. They will tell me that it looks very Eastern, or at least they know that it's not Western, but can't say for certain why that is. This shows that they are able to see the traditional in the work: they can feel the cultural spirit. The importance of my work is whether or not there is something genuine in it. If there is, then the audience will be able to perceive it.

In 2000, I exhibited a work in Europe: I used paper, six to seven meters long and one meter wide. I used smoke and soot to "paint" on the paper. In total, there were twenty or so pieces. Hung together, they resembled a screen that had been burnt by a large fire. The European artists asked me if these materials were all brought over from China. I told them no, they were all from here. They then asked: even though it has been displayed in a Western way, why does it feel so Chinese? Although it's difficult to put into words, I felt that it was sufficient enough that that they could sense this.

I create in this way because it is what is most familiar to me; I grew up with it, so I know it better. Even in this age of globalization, I don't really understand what is "global." Is it what is prevalent in developed countries? Once, in Europe, when I gave a talk, a German sinologist asked me why I used this particular method for my art. I said, "You're a sinologist, and your mother tongue is German. When you really want to explain something clearly, what language do you use?" He answered, "Of course, I use my mother tongue." I said, "You're a sinologist, yet when you want to say something clearly and sincerely, you use German. I am the same way." When I use a foreign language, it is extremely difficult for me to express myself. The way I make art is similar. Even though internationalism and globalization are very fashionable right now, I don't consider myself in that way because I don't really understand it.

When I first began [making] art, I used paper for painting. But at that time, I didn't have the concept of paper that I have now. Paper is white, a blank slate; it has nothing on its surface. The process of painting on it or filling it with something is very interesting. But I think paper itself has its own meaning, too. Many developments throughout man's history have been accomplished through paper. Moreover, I feel that the way that Western people and Eastern people use paper and think about paper is different. In China, for example, when someone dies, we burn paper; it's used for paper-cuts, it can be used as a window pane, we often make things out of paper, etc.—it can serve many different functions. In the West, I feel that it is more associated with printing and writing.

If you use a piece of gold to make something, the material itself is very expensive. If you use a piece of paper, perhaps it doesn't have the same worth. But as an artist, I think that how you treat

Pl. 33. Qin Chong, *Birthday I*

the material determines its role. If you bestow paper with the value and ideas that you give to gold, then perhaps that piece of paper can be a piece of gold. If you don't bestow anything on the gold, then it just remains a piece of gold.

Since I first started using paper, I've also used smoke and soot. I take a piece of clean, white paper, hang it horizontally in the air like an awning, and then light a fire beneath it. People are always worried that I'll catch on fire. I wear a mask because of the black smoke. Fire seems like a very negative force: it's uncontrollable, leaves behind soot, and dirties the air. But when the piece is finally exhibited, people can't help but touch it because it looks too clean. Fire is associated with the origins of mankind, and it's contributed so much over the course of human history. Because people are so familiar with the uses of fire, it brings forth multiple meanings when they see my work. I feel that paper has a similar role. It is something that people are very familiar with and embodies its own depth and weightiness. So when people encounter my art, they are able to sense its content and connotations.

Pl. 34. Qin Chong, *Birthday II*

Based on an interview conducted by Peggy Wang in 2005.

▲ Pl. 35. Qin Chong, *Birthday III*

▼ Pl. 36. Qin Chong, *Birthday IV*

Qin Siyuan (Colin Chinnery, 1971–)

Born in Edinburgh, Scotland.
1997, graduated from the School of Oriental and African Studies, University of London.
Lives and works in Beijing.

秦思源

1971年生于苏格兰，1997毕业于伦敦大学亚非学院，现居北京。

A Self-Portrait Book, 2003
Chinese calligraphy paper (*xuanzhi*), thread
34.7 x 56 cm (13¾ x 22⅛ in., open); 34.7 x 31.6 cm (13¾ x 12½ in., closed)
Collection of the artist

我的书

宣纸，线

A Self-Portrait Book is a book made of traditional Chinese paper, *xuanzhi*, and also bound in a traditional Chinese format. It's part of a series of works I did on self-portraits, each exploring a different medium. I've used ice, objects like cubes, [and] photographs. I'm quite new at making artwork, so I thought maybe a good place to start is [with] myself, and [then] I can work my way outwards.

Inside the book are photographic details of my skin. They are photographed at very high quality, enlarged, and printed on *xuanzhi*. The *xuanzhi* is folded and bound in a traditional Chinese format, *xianzhuang shu*. The book itself, I guess, raises the question of narrative. A book is a very good way of exploring both narratives and self-portraits because it is, in a way, linear, whereas an art object is often non-linear. So a book is a good way of exploring oneself in a non-textual way.

Another thing is that the texture of skin is very interesting. When you blow it up, some of it looks almost like landscape; some of it is very specific and some of it is very abstract. If you were to put all of the pieces next to each other, you wouldn't concentrate on any one piece and would end up looking at the whole. So what you get is a kind of mosaic of different skin textures that would blur into one. This wasn't what I wanted.
I didn't want something to be in your face with flesh and skin. By leafing through piece by piece, one by one, the act of reading a book meant that you could spend time on each individual image. As you go through it, image by image, you see so many different textures. You try to identify what part of the body that [image] is and [how] that relates to oneself. So, even though you are looking at me, you are relating [the image] to yourself subconsciously. You can't help that, because you can only reference yourself. So another aspect of this is that as you're reading, it brings up funny references like "reading someone like a book." And yet obviously because it's just skin, because it's non-narrative, you're not reading anything really. You're just going through lots of different textures. Some of them are very enjoyable to view, and some of them are surprising because you didn't realize that you had so many textures in your skin.

I used a Chinese book and not an ordinary Western book format, which easily could have been the case. One thing about it was that a Western book is just too much like a catalogue: people take it for granted, flip through it like a catalogue, and don't treat it page by page. This is not to say that there aren't Western books that are just as much art objects as Chinese books. It really depends on how it's presented and displayed. If you just have it on a coffee table and have several strewn about, people will obviously treat it like it's just there to be flipped through. However, if it's on a pedestal in the middle of the exhibition hall, then it's different. It's very important for this book not to be treated like a catalogue. It's important that

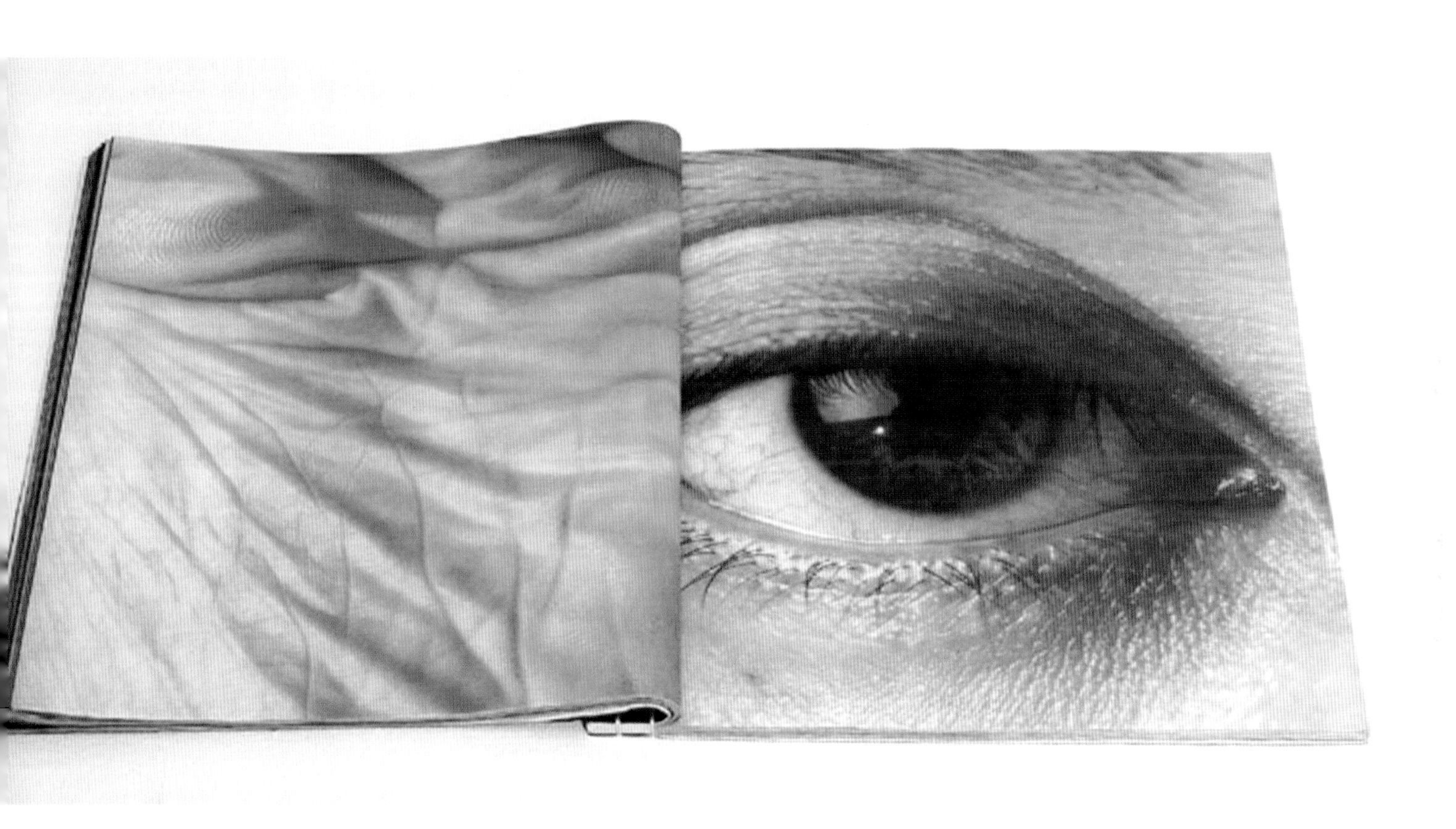

Pl. 37. Qin Siyuan, *A Self-Portrait Book*

this book is treated like an artwork. This is not because I feel this work is lofty or a terribly high work of art. It's simply so that people will approach it with a sense of "it's an artwork"; they will be more careful, look at it page by page, and absorb more of the work in it.

But the real reason is that *xuanzhi* is very soft and textured. You like the feeling of it on your fingers. It's almost like skin. And because of that as you flick through the book, you get the strange sensation that you're flicking through skin. And there's a kind of intimacy to it, but also a slightly strange sensation. But you only get that sensation if you treat it as an artwork and you see it carefully page by page. It's meant to be touched by the fingers; I hope that people don't have to wear gloves. I realize that in a very long exhibition, after a couple months, it might get destroyed. And that's a part of the book as well. It's a book that's meant to only last one exhibition. So each time there's an exhibition, I'll print a new book. I like that it's fragile, that it can get damaged, that it's not collectible really. These are all things I quite like about the work. I'd like to think that I'm being generous by allowing people to destroy my work.

I think there should always be work out there that is generous enough so that people can have the direct contact that they hardly ever get with a piece of work. Interactive art is not the same thing; it's almost like an IQ test where you are putting out all these challenges and people have got to interact with it. The act of reading through a book is just a part of your natural life. There is nothing contrived about it in its interaction with the audience. It's a very natural interaction that you do every single day.

My personal connection with this particular piece is in the format of the book. I used to work for the British Library on the Silk Road Manuscript project. All the books I worked on were from the fifth to eleventh century. The biggest and most important part of the collection was the collection of books from Dunhuang. The job was a cataloguing, conservation, and web project. One of the things I did during my work there was to write an article on the history of Chinese bookbinding based on the findings of the books in the Dunhuang collection. The article was meant as an educational tool so people could get a better understanding of why Chinese books are the way they are. It also took a look at the different kinds of inspirations that have been made into bookbinding. People don't think about this much because they always think that the Chinese had scrolls and later on we had books. But there were lots of explorations of how the whole thing evolved from one format to another, the scroll to the page; it's quite a big leap to make, and I wanted to show how it made that leap. I used examples from the Dunhuang collection to actually illustrate that. Most books throughout the rest of China have rotted away, so there's hardly any evidence apart from imperial collections.

I'm interested in the format of books anyway, and I've come into contact with Chinese books through my work. So, in a way, it's quite natural for me to use a Chinese format rather than some other format of a book.

Based on an interview conducted by Peggy Wang in 2005

Qiu Zhijie (1969–)

Born in Zhangzhou, Fujian province.
1992, graduated from Zhejiang Academy of Fine Arts.
Lives and works in Beijing and Hangzhou.

邱志杰

1969年生于福建漳州，1992年毕业于浙江
中国美术学院，现居北京和杭州。

Bookshelf No. 1, 2004/2006
Photography installation
180 x 276 cm (70⅞ x 108¾ in.)
Collection of the artist

未完成的书架1
装置，摄影

At the Visual Culture Center of the China Academy of Art in Hangzhou, we've been thinking of creating a set of books called *xingdong de shu*, "Action Books." It would be sold in bookstores, but the books themselves would be works of art. In reading the books, viewers would be able to participate in the art form, while there would also be mechanisms inside the books to further the idea of "action." I've always been interested in children's books, like pop-up books and books that have moving parts that you can lift and flip open to change. I often buy these types of books. In such cases, the books themselves constitute a type of place and space. For example, if there is a hole in the page, lifting up the page creates one meaning, while layering it creates a different meaning. These means of spatializing and temporalizing a book and adding to its inherent ideas and concepts interest me a great deal.

Last year, I made a work having to do with books: photographs of bookshelves filled with books. Whenever you go to a friend's house, you always look at their bookshelves. If you see a book that you yourself have, it gives a reassuring sense of security. If you see a book you don't even recognize, it elicits a sense of panic. To have similar books gives the sense that it is possible to communicate with this person. If you don't see any familiar books, it's like being lost in an ocean—suddenly stumbling upon a familiar book is like finding an island oasis.

These bookshelves have actually been manipulated in two ways. First, we changed the titles of some of the book to ones that don't exist. The work is very large, so this only becomes apparent upon close observation. However, there are so many books in the world that it seems possible that these books could, in fact, exist. After all, one can only have a limited knowledge of all the books in the world. In this way, the distinction between the real and the unreal becomes almost negligible.

We also combined many different people's books together onto one bookshelf—*manga*, texts on natural sciences, classical works, etc. The effect is an incomparably diverse and complex collection of literature. It's done to the degree that it would seem impossible for such an intellectually complicated person could exist. In this way, these photographic prints are like an unending handscroll; perhaps for one exhibit twenty meters could be on view, while for the next, thirty meters could be shown depending on the space.

I have another work that is related to books and printing. During the summertime in China, it is common to sleep on straw mats. I carved characters onto such mats in reverse, so that as people lay on them, the words would become imprinted on their backs. The earliest works have Mao Zedong's words, and in my most recent series, I carved excerpts from the *Shijing*. I photographed a row of people after they had lain on the mats; when they stood next to each other, the text could be read as a whole. The idea here is closer to the tradition of stele rubbings. A stele is one form of book. Because we want these words to be everlasting, we inscribe them onto stone. When imprinted on the body, however, the words vanish after a mere ten minutes. And yet, through photography, we can leave an indelible image. This process of transformation—appearing and disappearing—is closely related to many things.

In 2000 when I was in Japan to exhibit work, I was given a bicycle to ride. I covered one of the bicycle tires with a piece of tape, onto which I carved Chinese characters. These characters represented different rhythmic compositions and meters used in classical Chinese poetry: *ping ping ze ze, ze ze ping ping,...* Everyday, I rode this bike around town. When I passed through a puddle, the words would be visible. Although the bicycle was continually printing onto the streets, one could only see the inscriptions when I passed over water. On the last day that I was at the museum, I covered the tire with ink and made prints of these characters in the gallery.

I have also exhibited a *Blackboard* series, in which I photographed local blackboard announcements. I plan to make a book from these photographs. My original intention, however, was not to make art, but to conduct cultural research. These types of blackboard announcements are becoming more infrequent and will eventually disappear. In some areas, these announcements are being printed out and handed out to residents. In Beijing, I go around every month and photograph these blackboards. It's always different. Some say how to deal with SARS, some encourage people to donate money for tsunami relief efforts, [and] some report the meetings of the central government. I would like to bind these photographs together and create an annual record of blackboard announcements. I think it might be more appropriate to exhibit this in China or to print these as books to sell to local commoners. In some ways, there are many humorous things in here that are untranslatable.

The book that has had the greatest impact on me has been the dictionary. Ever since I was a child, I've repeatedly read the dictionary. Even these days, I continue to copy it, for example in my series *The New Shuo Wen Jie Zi Dictionary.*

Pl. 38. Qiu Zhijie, *Bookshelf No. 1*

A private collection of books always reflects the owner's mind and education. "Whenever you go to a friend's house," the artist says, "you always look at their bookshelves. If you see a book that you yourself have, it gives a reassuring sense of security. If you see a book you don't even recognize, it elicits a sense of panic. To have similar books gives the sense that it is possible to communicate with this person." What Qiu Zhijie presents here, however, is a fictional book collection that combines bookshelves from different homes. He has also changed the titles of books to imaginary ones. The result is an incomparably diverse and complex collection of literature which does not exist in reality.

—WH

Reading classical dictionaries allows you to trace your origins; you feel like you can see the most fundamental things. When you're done reading, it's like you've discovered everything, as if the whole world were only composed of these things. In *The New Shuo Wen Jie Zi Dictionary* series, I recorded groups of characters onto separate hanging scrolls; all the characters with a shared radical were written on the same scroll. If there were a lot of characters, I just wrote layers upon layers of them. It is fascinating because in this linguistic system, indexed by radicals, we can locate the basis of our entire conceptual structure. For example, there are hundreds of characters with the female radical. But there are only three based on the male radical (*nan, jiu, sheng*). I kept wondering why there was such a discrepancy. Then I realized that it shows how men, as subjects, have always discussed women, as subjects.

Sometimes I directly use books as materials, sometimes I use them to study the culture of the book, sometimes I use the book's content, or I look at how books emerge through the printing process. Thus my understanding of "books" is rather broad. This is very close to the idea of the "action" books that I discussed earlier: on one side is documentation and preservation, and on the other side is dissemination and communication. When does the image emerge, when does the information vanish, when does it reappear again—my interests have to do with these ideas. Perhaps my main focus of interest is in communications and the concept of communication. In the beginning when I studied calligraphy as a child, it [communication] had to do with calligraphy. Later when I learned printing, it adopted new meanings. I am interested in what occurs in this process of communication. From 1990 to 1995, I worked on the *Orchid Pavilion Preface*. Actually, at the time, I often copied the Heart Sutra for my own practice. I have an album at home of these copies. The Heart Sutra is only two hundred or so characters. However, on some pages it has been copied so many times that the page is now black, while on other pages, it is only copied once. In ancient times, Buddhist monks would copy scriptures, as the process of copying had to do with religious ideas of learning and internalization. After the popularization of printing, however, this practice of copying diminished.

Based on an interview conducted by Peggy Wang in 2005.

Song Dong (1966–)

Born in Beijing.
1989, graduated from Capital Normal University.
Lives and works in Beijing.

宋冬

1966年生于北京，1989年毕业于首都师范大学，现居北京。

A Room of Calligraphy Model Books, 1995
Installation; printed books
18.5 x 26.5 cm (17⅜ x 10½ in.) each book
Collection of the artist

碑房

装置，碑帖印刷品

For the work *A Room of Calligraphy Model Books*, I used scissors to cut the pages of calligraphy model books into strips of paper. Each strip is still attached to the spine, so that when the book is opened, it resembles a patch of grass. I placed these books together to give the impression of a grassy field. When I first exhibited this in 1995, it was shown in an apartment. In the corner of the room, I hid fans to blow wind over the grass. The room was sealed, so that viewers couldn't enter and weren't able to see the fans.

I exhibited this again in 1998, and then, in 2001, it was exhibited for Feng Boyi's show *Knowledge is Power*. This last time I used the same materials, but adopted a carpet-like form. I changed the theme because the exhibit was located inside a large complex of bookstores. Surrounded by all of these books, I decided to use the same materials to make a carpet of books that could neither be stepped on nor read.

During the Qing dynasty, a scholar wrote, "Gentle wind, you cannot read, so why do you turn the pages?" (*Qingfeng bushizi, hebi luan fanshu*). Because the character *qing* was used to describe the wind, it was interpreted to be a criticism of the foreign Manchu rulers. That scholar was subsequently put to death. This marked a time of great cultural persecution, in which words had the power to imprison a person.

In this work, the wind is reading these books. I like to change methods of reading to allow people to think more broadly. This work can be big or small, although exhibiting one book and exhibiting many books may elicit different reactions. If you exhibit just one, there seems to be a specificity as to which book has been cut up. But if you exhibit many, then the individuality of the book doesn't matter. Even in this more extensive view, however, they are all still stele rubbings bound into calligraphy model books. It's interesting because I don't even really know the content of these calligraphy model books. I've copied many different stele rubbings, but I have never read them as texts. I've chosen to use stele rubbings in this work because they are a way of transmitting knowledge. As a contemporary artist, however, I don't think that tradition is a bad thing, but rather something that can be utilized. Everything has its significance: if it can help me, then I will use it or accept its impact. But I do think that tradition has its problems, too. It can be confining and can limit your creativity. We need a new way of re-evaluating tradition. Even though the stele is the origin of this cultural transmission, I didn't shatter the stone into pieces. It is the publication of its rubbings that needs to be reformed. Over the years, people have copied these rubbings. Some people become geniuses, but most are circumscribed by tradition.

I actually really like books and even collect some. My love for books probably comes from my own experiences. During my childhood, books were considered poisonous things. I didn't like the books that they wanted us to read, but we weren't allowed to read the books that were of most interest to us. So I would secretly read them on my own, and they soon became something I really desired. My perception of books derives from the idea that too much knowledge comes from books. I feel that books can be a source of nourishment, but can also prevent you from moving forward. Sometimes, it can even be a poison.

My first work concerning books was a "book without words." For a solo installation, I had my students read these "books without words." I feel that if you read too much, then you start to develop particular attitudes. Maybe there are other perspectives from which to interpret books. Perhaps in taking away the words and starting from blank pages, one might still be able to read something. I've always considered having and not having as one and the same. When you read a book without words, you can still gain something. You don't come away with one or two lines, but rather end up reading yourself.

At that time, when I had my students read these books, it was as a performance. But then I started my own "book without words." I am the only person who has ever seen this book. Because I don't want anyone to bother me when I read it, I do it in private. No one, not even my wife, knows where I hide the book. On each page, I drew a rectangular frame, but there are no words inside. Every time I read it, I write on the margins the time at which I began. When I'm done reading, I write the time at which I finished. What does it mean to finish reading? When you feel like the time is up. Sometimes I read it for a minute, sometimes for half an hour. I began keeping this book in 1994 and have had it for eleven years now. I sit and read. When I read it, I feel like I'm reading myself. It's sort of like a form of deep meditation. I feel like I've created an object to help myself concentrate, and it's given me a great deal of help. When the margin of a page has been filled with the recording of times, then I move onto the next page. When the margins of all of the pages have been filled, then the book is finished. Even over the course of more than ten years, I have yet to finish reading this book.

This is my favorite work. The works that I like the most are the ones that I never exhibit, because they are the ones that are most purposeful in my personal life. For example, although I've exhibited photographs of my "Water Diary," I have never exhibited the diary itself. I rarely talk about them because they are a method for personal reading. They affect my daily conduct. This book is a medium through which I can focus my energy. It allows me to procure something, which I think is the goal for

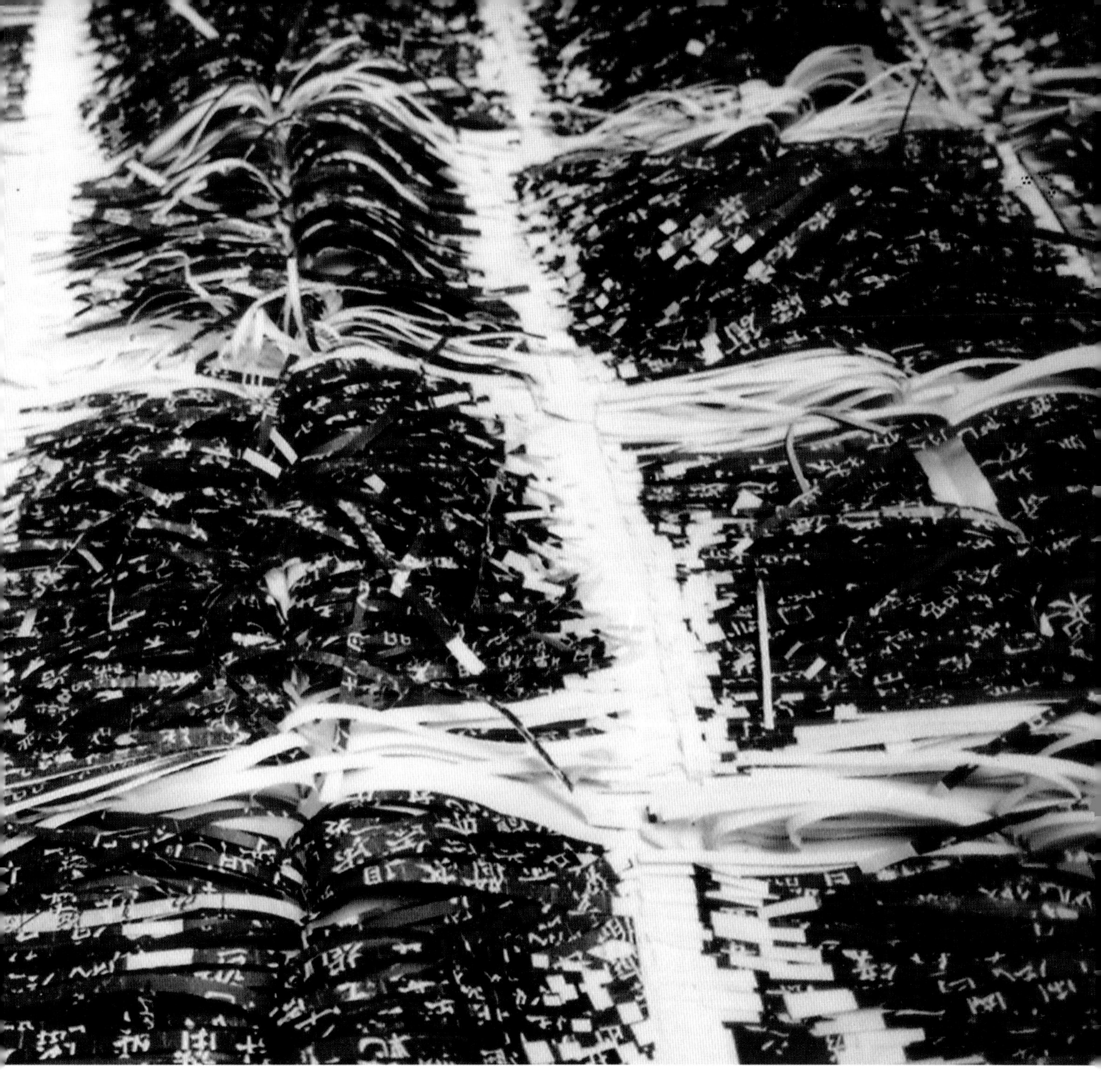

most books. What I gain from this book is no less than what I learn from books with words.

I believe that after reading a book, one shouldn't be limited by it. You should reap its contents and then forget it. This is not to say that you don't know the content or have destroyed it, but rather you have applied your own individual creativity to absorb and understand it. You can digest it and use it as nourishment.

Based on an interview conducted by Peggy Wang in 2005.

Pl. 39. Detail of Song Dong, *A Room of Calligraphy Model Books*

Wang Jin (1962–)

Born in Datong, Shanxi province.
1987, graduated from Zhejiang Academy of Fine Arts.
Lives and works in Beijing.

王晋

1962年生于山西大同，1987年毕业于浙江中国美术学院，现居北京。

New Ancient – Stele of Zhang Qian, 1998
Polyvinyl chloride (PVC)
56.5 x 36 x 3.3 cm (22¼ x 14¼ x 1⅜ in.)
Collection of the artist

新古今
塑料

My book *New Ancient – Stele of Zhang Qian* is made up of printings of stele rubbings on PVC. In total, I printed ten books, but each book is ordered differently. I produced these ten books in 1998 and exhibited them in Fukuoka, Japan. The ten were exhibited in different public spaces within the city: for example, a bookstore, a street, a library. In some places we put one; in others we put two. In one instance, one book was even wrapped in plastic and placed in a pushcart. Now, some are in the hands of private collectors and institutes, and I only have one or two left. Actually, I don't think that there is much difference between exhibiting one and exhibiting ten. The meaning of the work isn't located in the quantity of books on exhibit, but rather lies in the transparency of the medium. When light passes through the book, one can see from the front cover to the back. Some parts of the book are entirely transparent. This is due to holes in the original stele rubbings where pieces have worn away or broken off. The making of a traditionally bound book with PVC makes apparent the visual connections between the front and back sides of each page. You get a sense of its layering and are given a sense of perspective. Unlike other books where you can only see the content of a page one at a time, here you can feel the second, third, fourth pages. There is an impression of movement in this book. You feel like you can see, ever indistinctly, the layering and depth of these pages.

Concept is concept. Art is art. Concept, itself, is not art. The critical question is how to transform a concept into art. Only through transformation can one convey concepts like the rhythm and changes in society. For example, calligraphy is not enough to be considered as an art; it is merely a practice. To achieve art, it needs to be transformed. In this work, I have created art by transforming PVC into a book.

Traditionally, stele rubbings have been bound into books. On the surface, my PVC book takes the same form as these traditional books.However, the words in traditional books convey specific information and communicate certain meanings. Yet, in my work, the content is no longer important. I have copied the words and the form, but my books cannot be read. Although it can be opened, I prefer that a viewer not flip through it. It's not a book to be read, but a book to be felt.

There are so many books today that cannot be read. Books are an industry, and reading them isn't important. Reading a book is like eating a hamburger. It's okay not to eat a hamburger, and it's okay not to read. This is not a society that needs or depends on books. In my own life, I don't read that many books. I prefer to listen to other people discussing books; I feel that this is a better way of receiving information. Books do help a person improve, but I feel that there are other sources from which to learn. Throughout your life, there may only be one or two books that you will ever really be able to read. After that, you may not be willing to read at all. It is a pity if one depends on books as a tool for survival or uses them as a place onto which to project one's thoughts.

When viewers see my work, they might feel like this is something that they encounter everyday and, therefore, not feel anything special towards it. This is, in fact, the feeling that books elicit from us nowadays. Everyday, people are flooded with books and information and are forced to passively

Pl. 40. Installation of Wang Jin's *New Ancient — Stele of Zhang Qian* on city street

accept them all the time. In an exhibition, however, viewers actively seek out what is most interesting to them. So when they walk by my work, they might not take much notice of it. But upon walking around, they might think back to it and find it interesting.

Books are also extremely stubborn. Even if you don't read them, they are still there, challenging you. Books have a certain ambience about them. Even without reading a book, you can feel it. It's like a magnetic field. I feel that the natural properties of PVC and books are very similar. They are both stubborn. They will not decay over the course of hundreds of years. Wood, metal, and paper will deteriorate over time, but PVC will not. It might change in color or texture, but it will still be there. Books, too, possess these properties of preservation and continuity.

Based on an interview conducted by Peggy Wang in 2005.

Wei Guangqing (1963–)

Born in Huangshi, Hubei province.
1985, graduated from Zhejiang Academy of Fine Arts.
Lives and works in Wuhan, Hubei province.

魏光庆

1963年生于湖北黄石，1985年毕业于浙江中国美术学院，现居湖北武汉。

Black Covered Book: Desert Storm, 1990–91
Paper-mache and mixed media
53 x 75 cm (20⅞ x 29⅝ in.)
Collection of Hanart TZ Gallery, Hong Kong

黑皮书：沙漠风暴

混凝紙漿，综合材料

Yellow Covered Book Series, 1990–91
Paper-mache and oil on board
3 books: 38 x 46 cm (15 x 18⅛ in.) each
Collection of Hanart TZ Gallery, Hong Kong

(1) *Yellow Covered Book: Crucifix*
(2) *Yellow Covered Book: Adam & Eve*
(3) *Yellow Covered Book: Car-Man*

黄皮书系列

混凝紙漿，板上油画

（1） 黄皮书：耶稣受难
（2） 黄皮书：亚当与夏娃
（3） 黄皮书：汽车人

Contemporary painting exceeds the boundaries of traditional art, and is no longer limited to any materials. The wide choice of materials enjoyed by the contemporary artist presents him with a wider range of possibilities: in other words, with free choice, which enables him to transcend previously accepted limits and functions, and frees him from the oppression of stereotypes. We are encouraged by our freedom to pursue questions that interest us, problems of cultural relevance, which make our art more vital. It is imperative that art create new forms not only by reexamining its own internal development, but by dealing directly with questions of contemporary culture. Only in this way can it make an impact on history.

From *China's New Art, Post-1989* (Hong Kong: Hanart TZ Gallery, 1993), p. 54.

In the early 1990s, artists' attitudes began to lean towards a sense of individualism, particularly after the First Guangzhou Biennial. "Pop" emerged in Wuhan, beginning a strand of art that would give rise to the greater contemporary Chinese pop trend that swept across the country. The art critic, Li Xianting...designated my art as "political pop." Other media sources saw my art as developing along cultural lines, and so also regarded my work as "cultural pop"...

My work at that time can best be characterized by the *Red Wall* series. I believe that after China's opening and reform movement, people's virtues and morals suffered greatly. I understood this suffering to be a decay of morals and sought to employ traditional Chinese moral stories and lessons as a remedy. I believed that these moral lessons preserved content that contemporary people had long forgotten. Although there are some vestiges that should be dispensed with, there are still aspects that are

Pl. 41. Wei Guangqing, *Black Covered Book: Desert Storm*

worth reviving. This also corresponds to the most basic principle of "Pop" art. "Pop" art originated in England and later developed in the United States; it formed an organic whole with economic, media, and market cultures. But China's cultural history is long and marked by an intrinsic independence. I feel that this should be more strongly emphasized. The distinction between my "Pop" and Western "Pop" can probably be located here. When making my art, I first focus directly on how we are limited by our familiarity with oil painting. For example, if we assumed that painting should be three-dimensional—that it cannot be a flat surface—then a new thing would emerge. This is turning the unbelievable into the believable...

During this time, I also experimented with other methods for expressing my thoughts. An artist can't only rely on using familiar methods to conform to ideas, but rather should consider using the most "suitable" method for expressing these

To many avant-garde Chinese artists, books cannot avoid being used by political and religious authorities to advance their ambitions. A grave lesson they learned from the Cultural Revolution is the alarming capability of a single set of books to control millions of people. Books are full of lies, and are also battlegrounds of different politics, religions, and ideologies. This dark side of the book is the central theme of Wei Guangqing's works shown here. In **Black Covered Book: Desert Storm*****, a metal apparatus on the left page contains photographs of Saddam Hussein and George Bush, commanders in chief of the first Gulf War. Miniature warriors and military vehicles are scattered around, covering the rest of the pages. Fifteen years after this book's creation, we can now better appreciate the artist's prophetic vision: as the revived war in Iraq drags on, this "black book" made in 1991 continues to comment on current international politics.***

—WH

Pl. 42. Wei Guangqing, *Yellow Covered Book: Crucifix*

ideas. Oil painting is fine, installation is fine; whichever language is appropriate should be used. But regardless of whether it is an installation, multi-media, [or] on a flat surface, I will still maintain a stylistic continuity, or a "similarity" in terms of pictorial language...

Last year, I produced the series *San zi jing* [Three Character Classic]. At their earliest, Chinese characters were related to forms. Therefore, I tried to restore these "characters" to this original sense of form. At the same time, I thought about how to relate the narrative of the *Three Character Classic* back to "characters" and somehow merge the two...I have tried to continue along one path for producing works: to connect the past with the present.

From Shen Wei, "Discussing *Red Wall* with Wei Guangqing," interview conducted February 2005, published on the internet by Tom Online, Inc., http://arts.tom.com/1029/2005516-21260.html (accessed July 11, 2006).

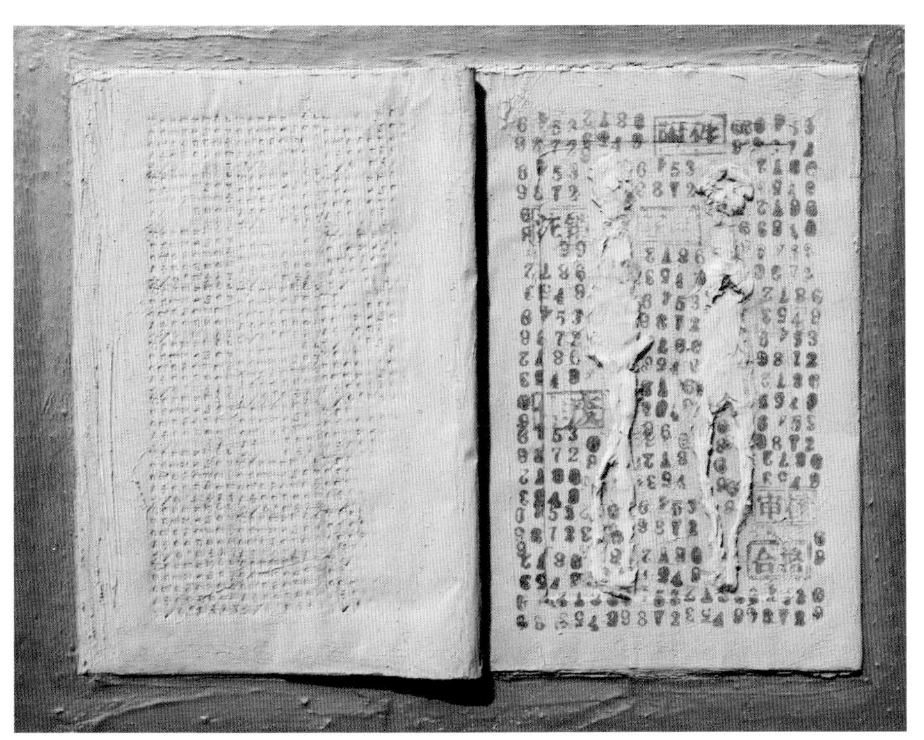

◀ Pl. 43. Wei Guangqing, *Yellow Covered Book: Adam & Eve*

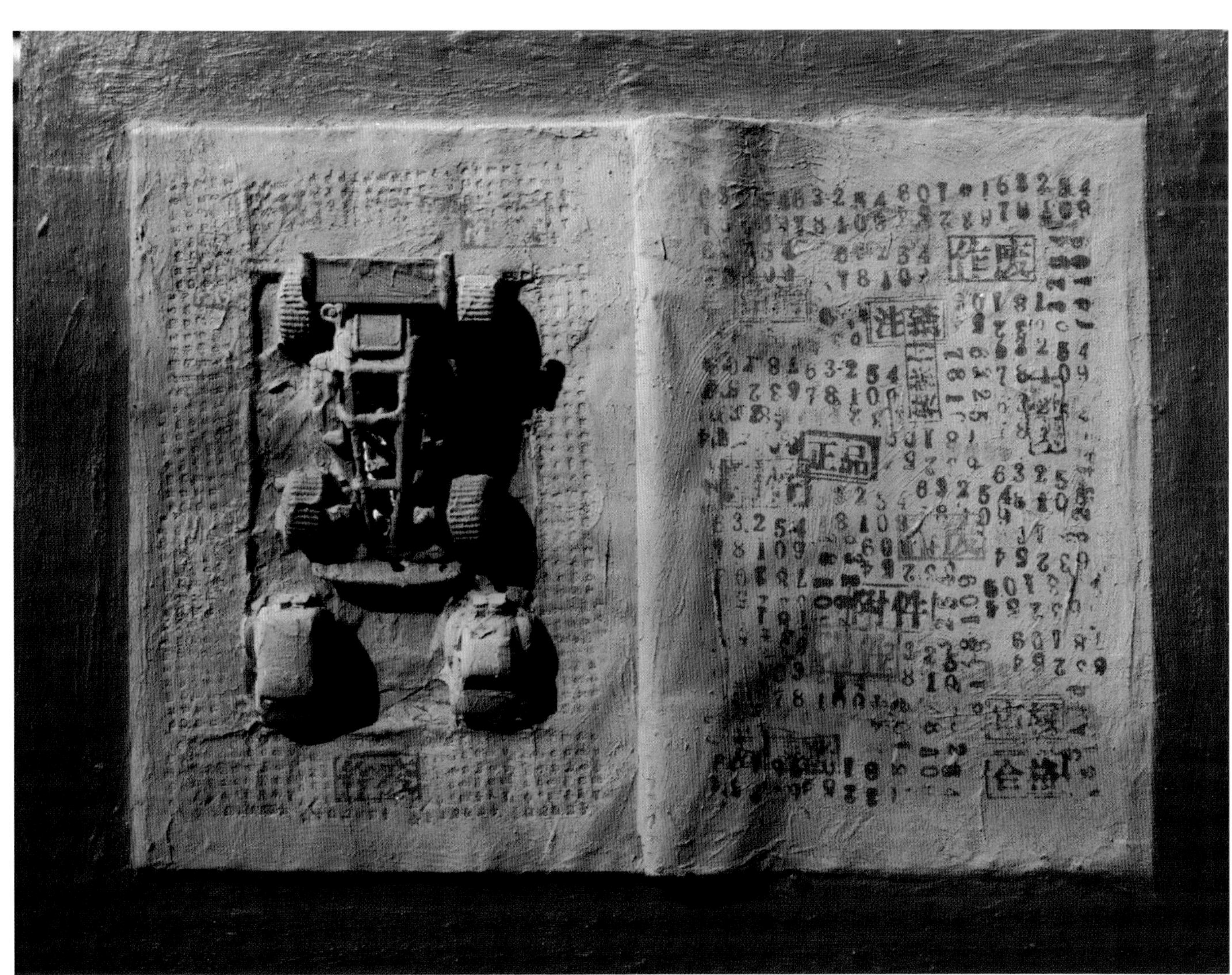

▲ Pl. 44. Wei Guangqing, *Yellow Covered Book: Car-Man*

Xie Xiaoze (1966–)

Born in Guangdong province.
1988, graduated from Qinghua University, Beijing; 1991, MA from Central Academy of Arts and Design, Beijing; 1996, MFA from School of Visual Arts, University of North Texas, Denton, Texas.
Lives and works in Lewisburg, Pennsylvania.

谢晓泽

1966年生于广东,1988年毕业于清华大学,1991年毕业于中央工艺美术学院,获硕士学位,1996年毕业于北德克萨斯州大学艺术学院,获硕士学位,现居美国宾州。

Chinese Library No. 1, 1995
Painting; oil on canvas
76.2 x 106.7 cm (30 x 42 in.)
Collection of George Morton and Karol Howard

中国图书馆1号
布上油画

When I was a child, I spent a lot of time around my grandmother. Sometimes, whenever she got together with a few other old women from the neighborhood, she would open up a thread-bound book with yellowish pages and sing out loud old famous stories: emperors, the loyal and the wicked, and heroes and beauties. It was mesmerizing. My father was a director of a middle school in the countryside. It was probably towards the end of the Cultural Revolution, when I was around ten, that I saw old books accumulated in his office waiting to be destroyed; at that time people were urged to turn in books deemed bad—feudalist, reactionary, or poisonous. I could not help looking at some of them; I had no idea what they were, but I remember seeing a few very old, colorful picture stories that I really wanted to steal but did not dare to. In my mind, thread-bound Chinese books always carry something mysterious and forbidden.

Rows or stacks of "sleeping" books found on library shelves first appeared in my paintings in 1993. *The Library Series* is an ongoing project. I see books as the material form of something abstract. In most of these paintings, you don't see authors or titles, only traces of categorization and organization left by librarians. Books are presented as containers whose content seem inaccessible; the spines form an impenetrable wall in front of the viewer. I am not so interested in books as a symbol of knowledge, education, or enlightenment; it is how the endless accumulation of documents becomes another existence or another world and the almost toxic air of decay that fascinates me. I am interested in the feeling of absence, impermanence, and loss in these images.

In the *Chinese Library Series* (1995 to present), I've painted thread-bound Chinese books with worm-eaten pages. In fact I was once referred to in an exhibition review as a bookworm. A bookworm who is always "digging into stacks of old papers" (*zuan gu zhi dui*), I have a long-standing interest in time, memory, and history—a thread which runs through my work. While I continued to paint Chinese and Western books, I also started in 1994 to make installations based on documentation of historical events; some of them have to do with the destruction of books, such as *Nocturne: Burning of Books by the Nazis* (1995) and *Order (the Red Guards)* (1999). Eventually my subjects expanded to include newspapers. In the paintings of stacked newspapers with fragmented news photos and texts (1998 to present), I attempted to combine my interests in the library and the perception/interpretation of history and politics in a simple format. My most recent project, *The MoMA Library* (2005–06), also deals with history: it engages very specific art-historical references. Over the years, things seem to have

Pl. 45. Xiaoze Xie, *Chinese Library No. 1*

opened up from books; formal, architectural, narrative, conceptual, and political elements seem to come together in the theme of the library.

I think that the development of each individual is greatly influenced by the larger social and cultural background, and one's experiences involving books, to some degree, shape one's view of art and life almost unconsciously. In my work, I rarely have any specific references to certain books or ideas in them. The accumulation of books has an architectural presence, but they are also banal and fragile. I focus on their qualities as ruins. I realized that books, even newspapers, have eventually become relics. To me, the disintegrating pages and the fragility of books seem to suggest the vulnerability of memory and history; the images that at times dissolve into abstraction suggest a sense of impermanence and loss. I hope my work is ambiguous and open to different interpretations by the audience, not just a didactic statement.

Personal communication between Xiaoze Xie and the curator.

Xu Bing (1955–)

Born in Chongqing, Sichuan province.
1987, received MFA from Central Academy of Fine Arts.
Lives and works in New York.

徐冰

1955年生于重庆,1987年毕业于中央美术学院,获得美术硕士学位,现居纽约.

Book from the Sky, 1987–91
Wood blocks, ink and paper
Collection of the artist

(1) 4 volumes of books in wooden box
49.5 x 34.3 x 10.2 cm (19½ x 13½ x 4 in)
(2) Wood block for frontispiece
35.6 x 50.8 x 5.1 cm (14 x 20 x 2 in.)
(3) Wood block for interior
(13 x 10 x 2 in.)
(4) Wood block characters
1–2 cm (⅜–¾ in.) square

析世鉴 - 天书
书,木刻版,墨,纸

Introduction to Square Word Calligraphy, 1994–95
Stone and printed book
Stone: 55.9 x 25.4 x 5.1 cm (22 x 10 x 2 in.)
Book: 40.6 x 48.3 cm (16 x 19 in., open)
Collection of the artist

方块字书法入门
平版印刷

Silkworm Book II, 1994/2006
Installation; video projection on book
Dimensions variable
Collection of the artist

蚕书
装置,综合媒材

Tobacco Project, 2000
Installation; mixed media
Collection of the artist

(1) *Red Books*
Cigarettes printed with quotations from Chairman Mao
8.9 x 10.2 cm (3½ x 4 in.)
(2) *Matchsticks*
Matchsticks with printed text, 3 items
3.8 x 4.5 cm (1½ x 1¾ in.) each
(3) *Tang Poem*
Tang poems printed on cigarette papers, 3 items
5.1 x 6.4 x 1.27 cm (2 x 2½ x ½ in.) each
(4) *Double Calendar Book*
Book made from cigarette packaging & pages of Xu Bing's father's medical records
12.7 x 19.1 cm (5 x 7½ in.)
(5) *Dao de jing*
Printed text on paper
2.5 x 58.4 cm (1 x 23 in.)
(6) *Reel Book*
Wood structure, printed cigarette paper
50.8 x 61 x 30.5 cm (20 x 24 x 12 in.)
(7) *Miscellaneous Book*
Hinged wooden boxes
30.5 x 20.3 x 2.5 cm (12 x 8 x 1 in.)
(8) Design of *Tobacco Book*
Paper
20.3 x 27.9 cm (8 x 11 in.)

烟草计划
装置,综合媒材

(1) 毛语录
(2) 火柴书籍
(3) 唐诗
(4) 双面日历册
(5) 道德经
(6) 回文书
(7) 杂书卷
(8) 达勒姆草图

From the materials to the design to the production process, every aspect of the *Book from the Sky* (see p. 8, fig. 2) was done with great earnestness. Every character was carved, hand-printed, and strictly installed into place. You can't help but think that this book must have some sort of deep meaning; why else would someone conduct this [project] with such seriousness? In reality, it does not have any content to tell you. But I believe that this work needs to be carried out very seriously; the greater the seriousness of the work, the stronger [is] its artistic power. If you randomly write a character or a composition, people will think it's a joke and that anyone can do this. But if you carve and print these characters with great earnestness, its artistic power is increased. In fact, there isn't a correlation between how good a work of art is and how much time and energy you spend on it. But in *Book from the Sky*—and in *Introduction to Square Word Calligraphy* to a degree—the level of earnestness is a language for art: it gives strength to artistic power. The form and methods that one uses are for reaching a goal, a specific idea.

Pl. 46. Detail of Xu Bing's installation *Book from the Sky*

Pl. 47. Wood block for interior text of Xu Bing's *Book from the Sky*

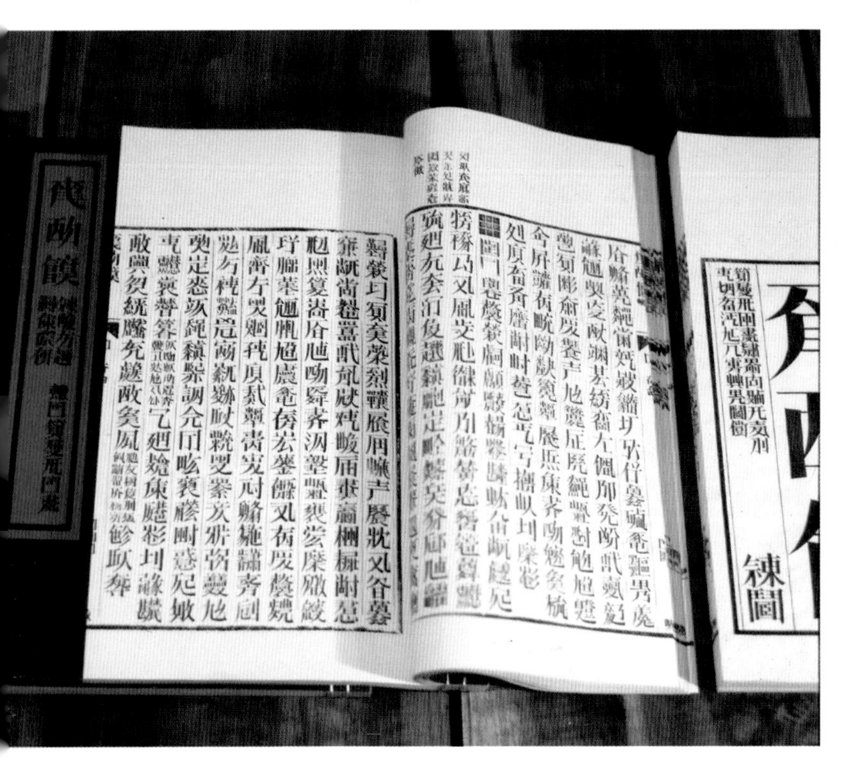

Pl. 49. Open book from Xu Bing's *Book from the Sky*

Pl. 48. Wood block for frontispiece of Xu Bing's *Book from the Sky*

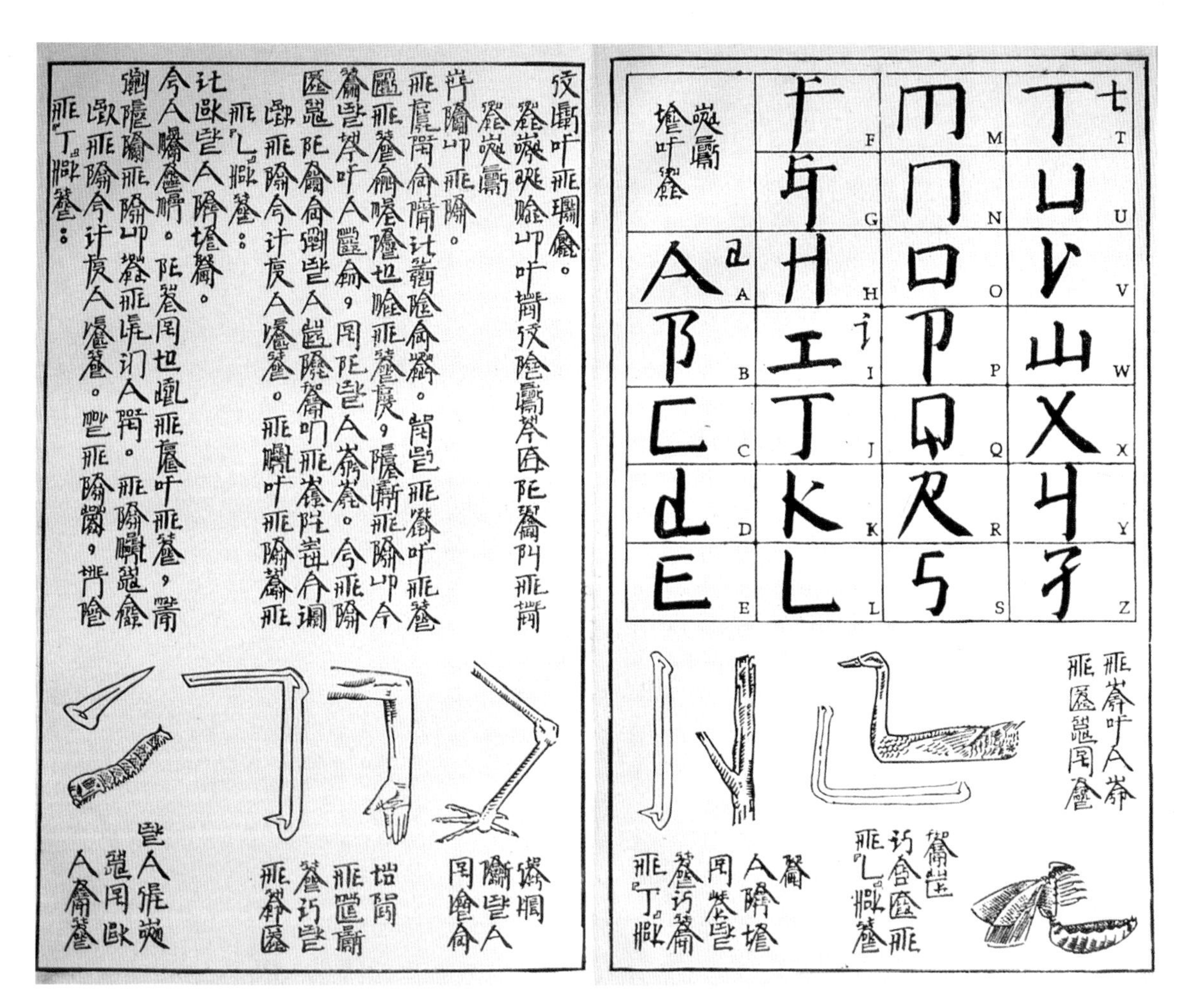

Pl. 50. Two-page spread from Xu Bing's *Introduction to Square Word Calligraphy*

Although nowadays we have computers, there is a sense of comfort derived from paging through books. Even if you don't carefully read the text, there is something comforting about browsing through the pages. This is a habit shared by everyone. Every time you turn a page, you open up a new space. There is a sense of vastness in there. Artworks concerning books utilize this aspect—the essence—of the book. They're not about changes in Chinese society or other such topics; they're about how to tap into this essence: what the relationship between the pages is, how you use the space on the pages, how text is aligned on the page, etc. When the *Living Word* was transformed into book form, I was able to insert a real dictionary there and have the words fly out of its pages. This is a feeling that is specific to a book and can't be achieved in an installation. In a book form, you can develop this sense of spatial limitlessness in the pages.

My generation has a very awkward relationship with words and books. In my personal experience, for example, I grew up in a culturally rich environment because of my parent's employment. Both of my parents worked at Beijing University, so I spent a lot of time at the library there. Because they were often very busy, they would let me stay in the library stacks. I was very young at that time, though, and I couldn't read any of the books. I would just page through the reference books, for example, texts on bookbinding, calligraphy styles, typesetting, the history of books, etc. I would also look at the different ways in which books were bound. I became very familiar with the books' exteriors, although I didn't know any of their contents. By the time of the Cultural Revolution, I could read, but there weren't any books available. The entire country read one book: Mao's "Little Red Book." We read and memorized that book all day. At the end of the Cultural Revolution, I returned from the countryside to Beijing to study. Because I was starving for culture and was in the midst of the general cultural fever at the time, I read so many different types of books. But after reading so much, I didn't feel well. It was like being overstuffed. It was at that time that I made *Book from the Sky*. It's the very awkwardness of this relationship with books and words that drew my interest to this subject.

I came to the United States when I was thirty-five years old. I didn't know any English at that time. Although my thoughts were mature, my level of language, communication, and reading made me illiterate. When I first came to the United States, I stayed at the University of Wisconsin at Madison. I was so surprised that they let people into the library stacks to browse and touch the

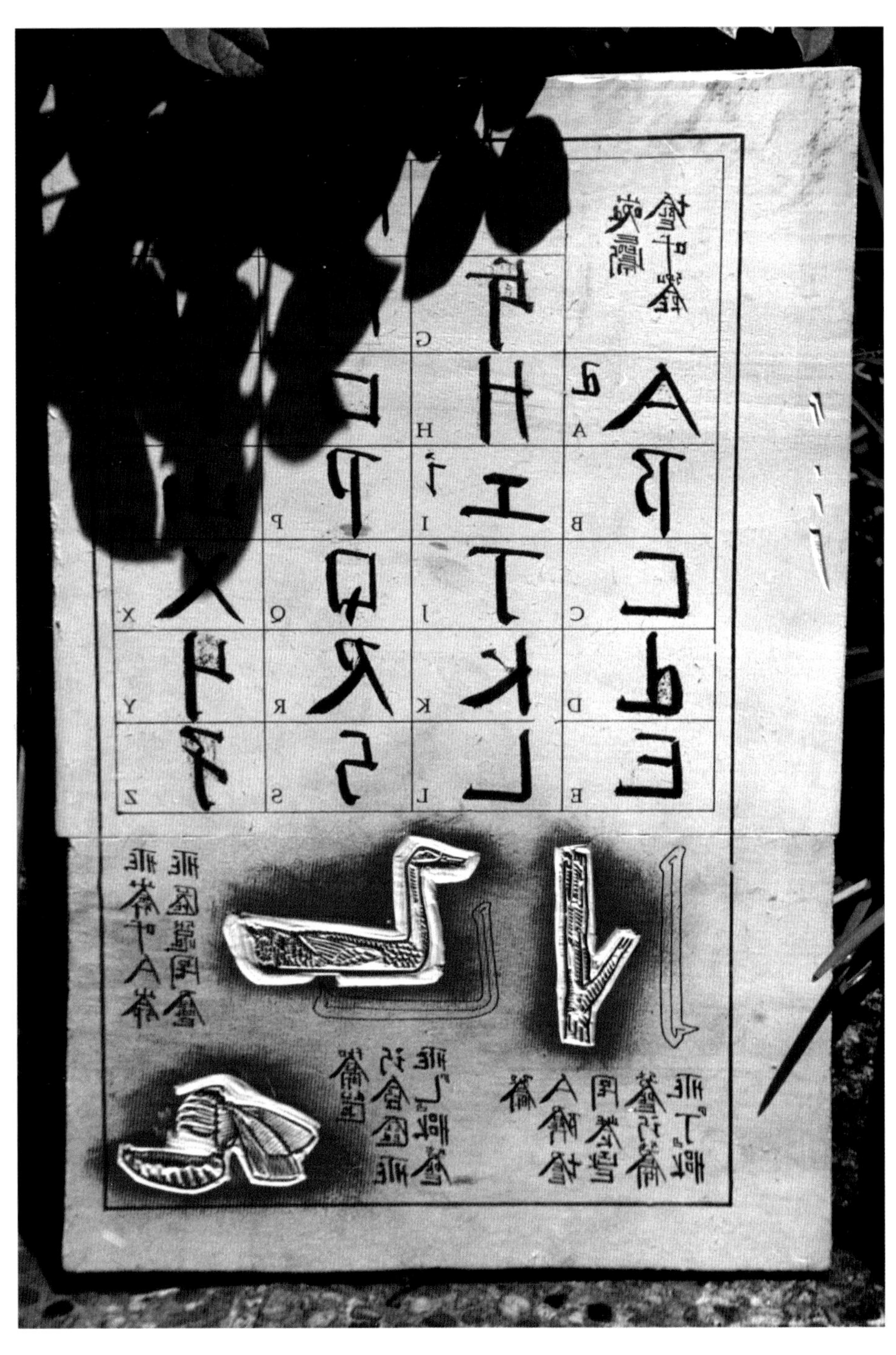

Pl. 51. Stone for printing Xu Bing's *Introduction to Square Word Calligraphy*

Pl. 52. Xu Bing, *Silkworm Egg Book*

books. I liked to go there and look at the books, but it was like I had returned to that earliest period in my life at Beijing University. There were so many books, but I couldn't read any of them! My generation has never had a normal relationship with books. When we should be learning to read, there are no books. When we can't read, we are surrounded by books.

Added to this are our experiences during the Cultural Revolution. Before, I had discussed my personal background. But the Cultural Revolution, the movement to simplify Chinese characters, big-character posters, and slogans—these are all shared by my generation. Because of my family background, I participated in a lot of propaganda activities in order to redeem myself and show my revolutionary spirit. During the Cultural Revolution, people who knew how to write and draw were valued because they could be used as tools for propaganda. After I made my works, people were surprised and said, "Xu Bing's calligraphy is quite good!" On the one hand, I received training from my family, and, on the

This work restages Xu Bing's* Silkworm Egg Book*, an earlier performance project during which silkworm moths laid eggs on the blank pages of a book, and the eggs hatched into thousands of tiny silkworms. In the current installation, the stained book functions as a "screen," onto which a video of the silkworms' metamorphosis is projected. In so doing, this installation represents a past performance in real time, but also translates an actual event into a visual representation.

The ancient Chinese are credited with the invention of sericulture—raising silkworms and manufacturing silk from their cocoons. Chinese literature and art is full of images of and allusions to silk making. Partly inspired by this tradition, Xu Bing created a series of works in 1994 and 1995, using silkworms to produce various kinds of patterns, textures, and movements. In these works, mature silkworms moved gracefully over books and computers while spinning shiny silk; silkworm eggs formed a raised-dot texture reminiscent of braille; and the tiny, black larvae crawled over book pages to generate the visual illusion of nomadic "words."* Silkworm Egg Book *was one of these fascinating works.

—WH

◀ **Pl. 53. *Red Books* from Xu Bing's *Tobacco Project***

Xu Bing created these "books" for his Tobacco Project, held in 2000 in Durham, North Carolina, the center of the American tobacco industry since the nineteenth century. The focus of the project was James B. Duke (1865-1925), the famed Durham tobacco tycoon, whose company was the largest cigarette producer in China in the early twentieth century. Each "book" shown here uses a specific image related to the cigarette, including Duke's company's advertisements in Shanghai, the design of Chairman Mao's favorite cigarette, as well as excerpts from Mao's writings, the Daode jing, and Tang dynasty poems. These works are "polycentric" in both content and image: Xu Bing neither planned them as a coherent visual display nor pursued a consistent social or political theme. Instead, tobacco inspired him to create these "books" as disparate objects, each pointing to a specific memory or meditating on the implications of the cigarette for modern Chinese history.

—WH

other hand, I received a lot of training during the Cultural Revolution. These attitudes towards books and the power of words are all reflected in my later works.

I have always been extremely interested in the relationship between characters and pictures. To what extent is the written word, in particular the Chinese character, communicated as a symbol? How is it used as a symbol? What component of this functions visually?

When I was little, my father would have me copy a page of writing everyday. In the beginning, I would trace characters and then later would copy them according to such manuals. At the time, I thought that he had me do this so I could write my characters well. But then I realized that this Chinese cultural system wasn't just a way for improving one's writing, but rather a method of cultural training. Its purpose was to raise a child according to a specific traditional Chinese system. This is a way of studying and researching culture. I don't think that there is any harm to this method. In fact, it's a method to let you better concentrate. It allows you to enter into this cultural system and grasp its essence. In this way, it is both fundamental and effective.

When I painted outdoors for my *Landscripts* series, I used characters to show natural changes. I began this series first when I was in the Himalayas. In the sketches, I tried to use characters to show the changes in the clouds, lightening and darkening, the moving fog, etc. It is very difficult to show the changes with these characters. It is at those times that you realize how difficult it is to express reality using concepts and symbols. But as one faces the mountains and writes/paints the character *shan*, it feels as though you can leap over everything having to do with history, painting, and calligraphy. Writing and painting *shan* become the same thing, and you begin to feel that those discussions in art history about style no longer have any meaning. What is style? It is this. It comes from here. You feel like you can touch something very essential within our culture. Why do Chinese people have a certain way of thinking or a certain aesthetic appreciation? Why is our furniture designed in such a beautiful and minimalist manner? It is very much related to our written characters. For example, when you see a window frame, you think of the Chinese characters *chuanghu*, because the characters derive from the structure of the thing itself. This effect on our way of reading, our aesthetic appreciation, and our taste must be different from [that felt by] those who study English.

Pl. 56. *Double Calendar* Book from Xu Bing's *Tobacco Project* ▶

▲ **Pl. 54. *Matchsticks* from Xu Bing's *Tobacco Project***

◀ **Pl. 55. *Tang poems* printed on cigarette papers from Xu Bing's *Tobacco Project***

After producing *Landscripts,* I found that you could really locate where the differences in Chinese and Western cultures arose. I think that the greatest difference between the origins of Chinese and Western cultures can be found in their respective written languages. In my *Landscripts,* landscapes are all composed of characters: rocks are *shi,* bamboo are *zhu,* [and]

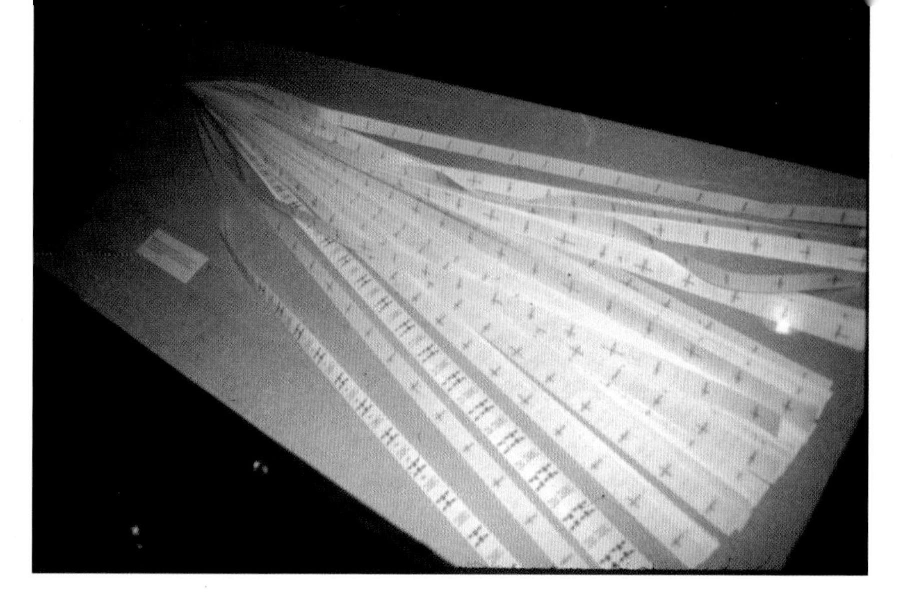

Pl. 57. ***Dao de jing*** **from Xu Bing's** ***Tobacco Project***

water is *shui*. Is this calligraphy, painting, or a piece of writing? It is all of these and none of these at once. It is the boundary that lies between things that is most interesting to me. For example, the work *Living Word* begins on the ground with the dictionary definition of "bird," then turns into the simplified character, then the traditional character, then clerical script, standard script, and so on all the way until it becomes the pictographic character for "bird." It looks at the transformation between the concept of bird and the actual thing.

Pl. 58. ***Reel Book*** **from Xu Bing's** ***Tobacco Project***

When I was making this work, I thought about Joseph Kosuth's conceptual work *One and Three Chairs*, in which he presented the dictionary definition of "chair," a photograph of a chair, and an actual chair. I thought about making my work as a contrast to this piece. In Chinese culture, it would be different: the relationships between the concept and the actual thing would be blurred.

Most written words are used for communication, expressing ideas, etc. My characters, however, are realized by way of a lack of communication. They disrupt the way that one is used to viewing culture. *Introduction to Square Word Calligraphy* is a companion to the *Red-line Tracing book*. They were originally exhibited in a classroom-like environment as textbooks to teach people how to write these square words: they look Chinese, but are actually English. People ask me, "Are Chinese people mad that you made Chinese into English?" And I tell them, "Actually Chinese people are happy that I turned English into Chinese." They are somewhere in between, so it's hard to say definitively what they are. I like to find things that don't yet exist within the limits of people's conceptual imaginations. In other words, I would like to broaden their scope for thinking.

When one tries to make sense of these ideas, it opens up space for thought. In fact, there isn't much change to the languages. But when you change the structure of the strokes, people think there is a major transformation. They think it's unbelievable that one could write English in this way. This just shows how great the limits of

Pl. 59. *Miscellaneous Book* from Xu Bing's *Tobacco Project*

people's thinking are. My *Introduction to Square Word Calligraphy* uses a traditional way of explaining how to form each brushstroke: the body of the stroke shouldn't look soft like a worm's body; the "hook" should appear as strong as a person's arm; etc. In the back, there are rubbings from carved stone, which look entirely like old calligraphy manuals.

I used this format because it brings both a sense of earnestness and humor. Almost all of my books appear extremely serious. *Introduction to Square Word Calligraphy* looks like an important classical textbook on calligraphy that has been passed down to us over the years. But, in fact, the actual content is totally different: it is a book about modern English! The greatest existing contradiction is between outward appearance and inner content. It's like wearing a mask. It gives you something familiar or unfamiliar, but you can't figure out what exactly is going on. It attracts you to enter and read and at the same time prevents the possibility for entering and reading. Here, it stimulates and challenges your thinking.

Based on an interview conducted by Peggy Wang in 2006.

Pl. 60. Design of *Tobacco Book* from Xu Bing's *Tobacco Project*

Yang Jiecang (1956–)

Born in Foshan, Guangdong province.
1982, graduated from Guangzhou Academy of Fine Arts.
Lives and works in Heidelberg and Paris.

杨诘苍

1956年生于广东佛山，1982年毕业于广州
美术学院，现居德国海德堡和法国巴黎。

100 Layers of Ink, 1994–98
Ink and acrylic on *xuanzhi* paper, metal frame
50.8 x 48.3 x 25.4 cm (20 x 19 x 10 in.)
Private collection, courtesy of Chambers Fine Art

百层墨

水墨，丙烯，宣纸，金属框

Layers of Ink (*Vast Square*) is a conceptual work, related to time, space, and the material of ink. An important factor is repetition, the aspect of multiple layers.

From an e-mail interview conducted by Peggy Wang in 2006.

Pl. 61. Yang Jiecang, *100 Layers of Ink*

Yuan Chin-t'a (Yuan Jinta, 1949–)

Born in Changhua, Taiwan.
Graduated from National Taiwan Normal University, Taipei, Taiwan; received MFA from City College of the City University of New York.
Lives and works in Taipei, Taiwan.

袁金塔

1949年生于台湾彰化，台湾师范大学美术系毕业，纽约市立大学美术研究所硕士，现居台湾。

Piling Up Books, 2005
Ceramic, mixed media
48 x 65 x 35 cm (19 x 25⅝ x 13⅞ in.)
Collection of the artist

堆书

陶瓷，综合媒材

I have attempted to express those things in life that possess an innate nature that is "eternal" or "interesting": for example, aspects of human nature such as love, avarice, deception, selfishness, etc. In my ceramic books, I combine people, events, and things from different times and spaces together in order to convert the "irrational" into the "rational." This allows the work to attain an effect that is profound, ironic, humorous, etc. The *Book of Odes*, the *Songs of Chu*, Tang poetry, the *Records of the Grand Historian*, the *Zizhi tongjian*, Song poetry, etc.—these are all materials that are of great interest to me. These classical texts all serve to transmit and eulogize the love between men and women, simple and primitive feelings, investigations of ecology, the praise and criticism of politics, and history as a reflection of the present; they move and motivate me again and again. As such, I take concepts from modern art as a means for interpreting classical literature; it is all in an attempt to touch what is called the "essence of life." At the same time, I am attentive to the relationship among words as symbols, illustrations, and images. I ponder their role in the contemporary Information Age and the problematic course of their ebb and flow.

I read broadly and in great quantity, learning new things by reviewing the old. I utilize the ancient for contemporary purposes and process the two dialectically. I present my ideas by juxtaposing different times and spaces and bringing them into dialogue with each other.

Books have always been a source of nourishment for my creativity: they serve to both influence and change my work greatly. In the ceramic books, for example, I take the book directly as the form for my expression. I not only paint freely on its surface, but also engage with it three-dimensionally. At the same time, classical literature and history are also encompassed in my work as motifs. This, in turn, creates multiple layers of time and space. The juxtaposition of ancient and contemporary words and images produces a dialogue, lending an additional aspect of interest to the work.

The *Book of Odes*, the *Songs of Chu*, Tang poetry, the *Records of the Grand Historian*, the *Zizhi tongjian*, Song poetry, calligraphy manuals from various dynasties—these are all sources of reference for me. From these sources, the diversity of human nature and appearance, man's relationship to nature, and the vicissitudes of politics in history are all revealed. These are the topics of my ponderings and the objects of my expression. From reading these books, I believe that the essences of life faced by every generation of people are, in fact, similar. These experiences and events recur continuously in a cyclical manner.

Classical literature and historical books are of tremendous interest to me. By using images and words from ancient and modern times, we can make inquiries into the postmodern Information Age and...about the relationship among words as symbols, illustrations, and images. I also work on combining my ceramic books with other mediums

Combining painting and sculpture, Yuan Chin-t'a's ceramic books are encyclopedic in nature. Their painted, immobile pages show people, events, and images from different times and spaces, extracted from their historical contexts and constituting an independent body of knowledge. The effect is serious and ironic, profound and humorous.

—WH

Pl. 62. Yuan Chin-t'a, *Piling up Books,* 2005

and ready-made objects, for example, rice paper, cloth, mosaic techniques, stainless steel, wood, lighting, televisions, etc., allowing one to read these ceramic books in even more ways. I add visual, audio, tactile, and other dimensions in order to strengthen the work's level of affinity with the audience members' participatory senses and feelings.

The wisdom of the past is located in traditional "books." But how one can use the past in the present is what is truly vital. Thus I ponder how to transform and utilize ancient texts and present-day media.

Books have always been one of humankind's most valuable instruments for recording memories and information. Yet, I have always relied on my powers of "circumspection" and "speculation" when reading them. Thus when I am creating artwork, I bring with me heavy criticisms and deep considerations.

I hope that the audience is able to merge my work into their lives. I hope that they read it with a sense of humor and carefree attitude and that within their laughter [they] are able to think deeply, discover, and be enlightened.

Based on an interview conducted by Peggy Wang in 2006.

Yue Minjun (1962–)

Born in Daqing, Heilongjiang province.
1983, graduated from Hebei Normal University.
Lives and works in Beijing.

岳敏君

1962年生于黑龙江省大庆市，1983年毕业于河北师范大学美术系，现居北京。

Garbage Dump, 2005–2006
Installation; acrylic on reinforced fiberglass, old books
6 items and books: 50 x 70 x 80 cm (19¾ x 27⅝ x 31½ in.)
Collection of the artist

垃圾站

装置，玻璃钢彩绘，旧书

This work was originally titled *From the Recycling Center to the Studio*, but after I thought about it for a little while, I decided to simplify the title to *Garbage Dump*. The books used in this work were all retrieved from places where one can purchase old rubbish and trash. The wide range of books here hints at the enormous amount of cultural garbage present in modern society, all of which work to bind and fetter people's spirits. Many of these books have never been read. They range from reference books to vulgar texts; some are extremely serious, others are philosophical, and yet others are materials for teaching. Through the passage of time, perhaps after half a year, these books become obsolete and are tossed into the garbage.

From this piece, one can sense that books serve to circumscribe the spirit and, at the same time, are something from which one tries to struggle free. The six figures surrounding these books are happy, yet also exude a kind of frenzied excitement. People don't often experience this type of mood: a kind of unthinking and irrational condition. It is the exact opposite of those images that one always sees of scholars and their attitudes towards books.

I hope that this work exhibits a kind of plain and not overly embellished feeling. Because books have been around for thousands of years, people no longer care how to bind or design them or how their exteriors and interiors have changed. Nevertheless, books still have a pure and simple effect upon me. In the process of making these sculptures, even their measurements lean towards a simpler air.

Books are very important to my production process. I have always read a lot of books, and a lot of inspiration for my works is born from these books. I read many different types of texts, from economic to political and cultural, etc. After I absorb them, I can synthesize them, learn from them, understand them…and only then can I abstract what is useful. In my life, I've come across many books. Trying to locate the valuable ones, the ones that I can really understand, is not a simple task. To extract from this immense tide of books the meaningful ones, the ones that you rely on your own consciousness to understand, is extremely difficult.

Regarding this question of "reinventing books," I have not really changed the book itself. I have not altered the book's text, structure, or content. I've only clarified a certain line of thinking: in a person's life, books have their own existence and fate. Some books vanish, while others live on. Books, in the course of human history, also have their own self-selective filtering process.

Books are certainly a record of man's history, culture, etc. But when later generations read earlier written accounts, they invariably reinterpret and re-understand these materials. This process of "re-doing" something is a means of seeking content that is relevant, of breathing life into tradition, history, and books, and of re-examining

Pl. 63. Yue Minjun, *Garbage Dump*

what's valuable. One could say that when a person reads, he is able to re-interpret its content.

I hope the viewer is able to see that in our world full of books not all books have value. A lot is waste, garbage, trash. I am only trying to discuss this question: Why is it trash?

Based on an interview conducted by Peggy Wang in 2005.

Zhan Wang (1962–)

Born in Beijing.
BFA, 1988, and MFA, 1996, from Central Academy of Fine Arts, Beijing.
Lives and works in Beijing.

展望

1962年生于北京,1988年毕业于北京中央美术学院,1996年并于该院获硕士学位,现居北京。

New "Suyuan Rock Manual," 2006
Printed paper book (original) and steel book
26 x 16 x 4.5 cm (10¼ x 6⅜ x 1¾ in.) each
Collection of the artist
新《素园石谱》
纸书与钢书

I believe that the importance of this book project lies in the concept and method that it proposes, and not whether or not it can be actualized. I've thought about this project for a couple years now, and if I can just display this idea, then I will have attained my goal. While I would like to have this book printed at some point, the physical realization of it is only secondary.

My work, the *New "Suyuan Rock Manual,"* is based on a text from the Ming dynasty. The original *Suyuan shipu* is an illustrated compendium of strange rocks. It includes visual and textual information from the Song dynasty onwards, edited and collected during the Ming. Explanations of each rock's unique characteristics, origins, stories, and even poetic appraisals by literati are all recorded alongside of its image. Prior to making my own *jiashanshi* (ornamental rocks), I wasn't aware of this book. But now it has become the basis for a compendium of my own rocks.

Rock culture dates back to the Han dynasty and reached its peak in the Song. It began to slowly wane in the Ming and Qing. And to what extent has it declined today? Rock sellers and buyers now only see rocks as resembling animals and such, and only use the most basic way of discussing rocks. Although rock collectors may know about this book, it doesn't really have much relevance in today's culture. Rocks should be cultivated, placed with trees or plants, with other rocks, or in an interior space. The choosing and positioning of rocks is an art. But in today's culture, they're put in places without any of these considerations.

When I first began making these rocks, it wasn't because I was trying to uphold this old culture. In fact, I made them with a sense of irony to show the decline of culture. When I thought about this book, it occurred to me: I should make a rock manual, too. I've made a lot of rocks and sold a lot of rocks. I have their measurements, information on who purchased them, [and] the gallery sales records, and I could choose among all of them. This rock manual is in line with one of my original ideas. I discovered that there was an inescapable logic to the production of my works: after I made one type of rock, I had to follow it with a different type and then another new type, because every rock has a different form. When you choose to make different forms, soon you amass records of a whole variety of different rocks.

Ancient *jiashanshi* are like this, too, because each rock develops its own unique form. This is why there is this thing called Chinese rock culture. In nature, there are so many different types of shapes that even farmers also began to choose, collect, and buy rocks based on their own personal tastes. In this way, it came to have a democratic feel to it. It can be said that it reached its peak in the Song dynasty with Emperor Huizong, who collected tons of rocks to build a garden. When the Jin dynasty conquered the Song, the rocks were dispersed to different places and the garden destroyed. I believe that common people then adopted this imperial idea and collected in large

Pl. 64. Zhan Wang, *New "Suyuan Rock Manual"*

quantities. This manual exists because, in the Ming, people who were engaged in the culture of collecting thought it to would be of value.

Rock appreciation is actually very conceptual—it's not judged on the basis of form, but can, for example, be evaluated on how much it represents man's relationship with his environment. Many people won't collect traditional works, but will buy my contemporary pieces. They see my pieces from a conceptual standpoint. They don't understand traditional Chinese art, but understand that I am transforming something. I think of art as an entryway. Here, it is a path for understanding traditional culture. Art serves as a path: it attracts people and allows them to slowly understand more about the past. In my works, Westerners are forced to understand the traditional through the contemporary.

The content of the book would entail records of the lives of my different rocks. For example, if a piece is sold to a particular collector or a museum, I will pair a photograph of the work with some writings on its background. I would include matters that arose when I was making the piece, comments on its origins, [and] interesting critiques or dialogues that might have emerged when it was exhibited. This format, including the photograph, differs from ancient formats. In ancient formats, the rocks were illustrated using plain drawings, but this method wouldn't have any meaning for my works; only photographs would be appropriate. Then I would include the rock's background, interesting stories, and information on where the rock is located now. This would be the basic format. In painting, there is the *Mustard Seed Garden Painting Manual*. But, in general, in art discourse there doesn't seem to be much discussion of these types of manuals. Western art collectors study just one or two objects. In China, however, collectors—particularly rock collectors—collect all different types of objects and forms. While there is an [aspect of] economics to it, this type of "playing" with rocks is a type of cultural activity.

My interactions with collectors have been very interesting. For example, in America, there was a collector who was dying of cancer. He specialized in collecting conceptual art and wanted me to create a piece within two months so that he could see it before he died. I was very moved by this. That winter, I was extremely busy, but I worked on it quickly to produce it by January. The rock was placed in his garden for only a month or so before he passed away. Along with the rock, I gave him a copy of *Gong hai*, a video of a rock floating at sea. I hoped that seeing this video would give him a sense of comfort. Recently, I was in San Francisco because a museum there had acquired a very large work of mine. It turns out that this collector's younger brother was a member of their organizational committee. He said to me: "this is in return for your altruism." Every rock has its own life and story. Perhaps each event itself doesn't have much significance, but when they are compiled together as a book, the book becomes both a copy of tradition and the construction of a new idea.

I hope that in this work the audience can see that the sale of an artwork is not a simple matter of selling a piece after it has been completed. In ancient times, the study, purchase, evaluation, and collection of ornamental rocks were inseparable processes that constituted a cultural activity. It encompasses a sense of passion and spirit that distinguishes it from a strictly commercial activity.

There has always been this problem between art and the market. But the collection of ornamental rocks is more complex because ornamental rocks are original and natural. Furthermore, their collection is based on choices and ruminations, particularly based on the vitality that rocks bring to a place. Today, I have tried to *make* ornamental rocks. Although they adopt the same form as the original ornamental rocks, they use new materials. This makes them relevant to our contemporary lives. However, you need to still maintain this practice of collecting by the masses in order to make it into a culture. To only produce a couple of pieces merely showcases an idea, an experiment—this doesn't achieve the status of being a cultural activity. Creating the piece is the first step. The second step is to make it, like ancient ornamental rocks, as something collected by many people. The third step is to produce a compendium of rocks. When this is done, then I will feel that the artistic production has been completed.

Based on an interview conducted by Peggy Wang in 2005.

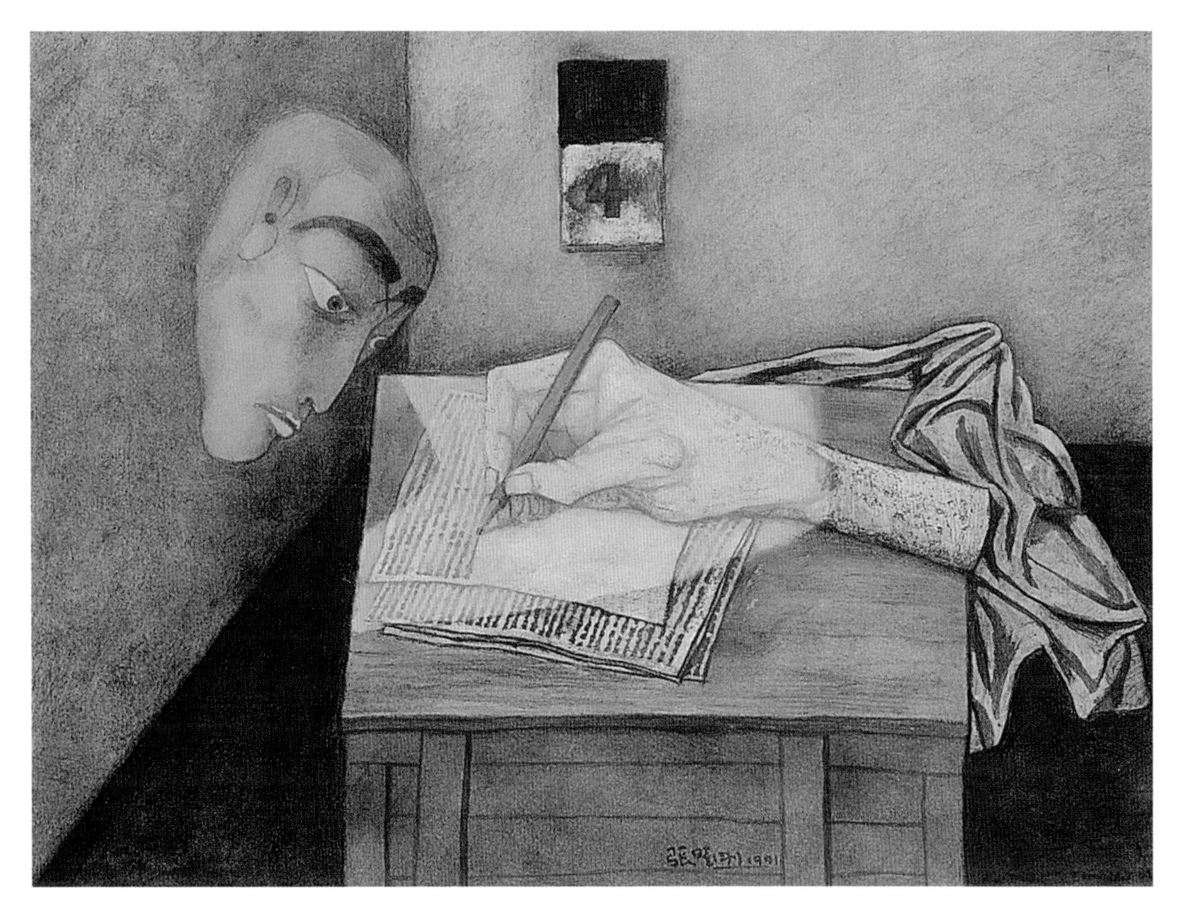

Pl. 68. Zhang Xiaogang, *Private Notes: Four, no. 4*

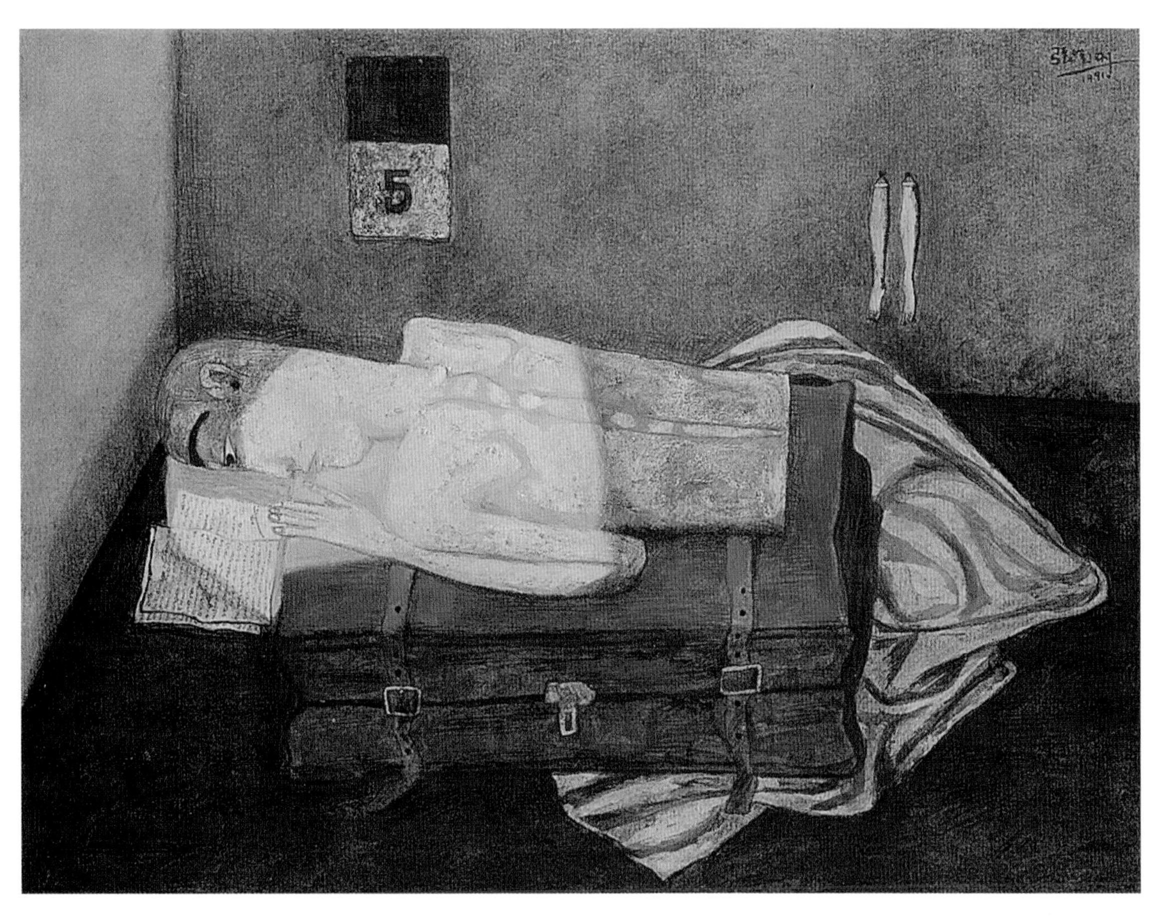

Pl. 69. Zhang Xiaogang, *Private Notes: Four, no. 5*

Pl. 70. Zhang Xiaogang, *Private Notes: Four, no. 6*

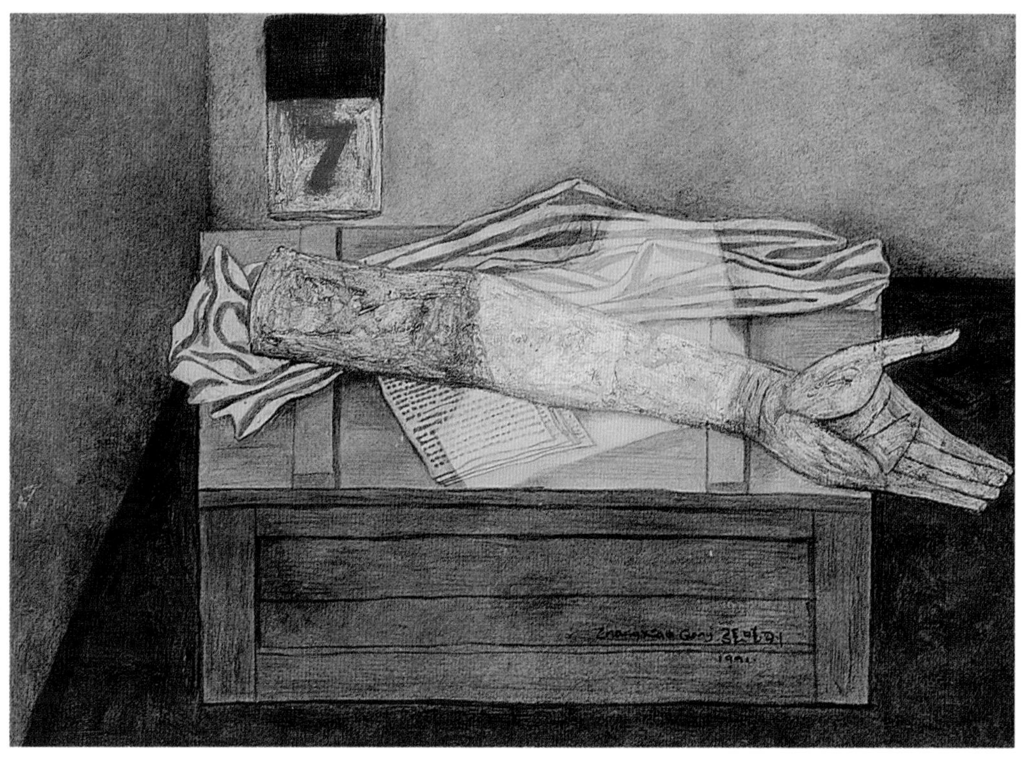

Pl. 71. Zhang Xiaogang, *Private Notes: Four, no. 7*

Pl. 72. Image from the series *Written Memories* by Zhang Xiaogang

Pl. 73. Image from the series *Written Memories* by Zhang Xiaogang

Selected Chinese Characters

85 Yishu Xinchao	85艺术新潮
badou	巴豆
ban bu lun yu zhi tian xia	半部论语治天下
Cai Guo-Qiang	蔡国强
Chen Xinmao	陈心懋
chuanghu	窗戶
Dao de jing	道德经
Dong Qichang	董其昌
Du wan juan shu, xing wan li lu	读万卷书，行万里路
Duobian de Laimenghu	多变的莱梦湖
Fang Lijun	方力钧
Fu Baoshi	傅抱石
furu	腐儒
Gao Jianfu	高剑父
Geng Jianyi	耿建翌
Gu wei jin yong, yang wei zhong yong	古为今用，洋为中用
Gu Xiong	顾雄
guohua	国画
Hong Hao	洪浩
Hong Lei	洪磊
Huachanshi suibi	画禅室随笔
Huang Binhong	黄宾虹
Huang Yong Ping	黄永砯
Huangjinye shu	黄金叶书
jiamian	假面
jiaoshu	校书
jiashanshi	假山石
jinshu	禁书
Lady Jiaoshu	女校书
Li Tinggui	李廷珪
Li Xianting	栗宪庭
Li Youlin	林有麟
Liu Dan	刘丹
Liu Haisu	刘海粟
Liu Yi	刘彝
Lü Shengzhong	吕胜中
manga (Jp)	漫画
mianju	面具
nan, yong, sheng	男, 舅, 甥
Pan Tianshou	潘天寿
ping ping ze ze, ze ze ping ping	平平仄仄、仄仄平平
pu	谱
Qi Baishi	齐白石
Qin Chong	秦冲
Qin Siyuan	秦思源
Qingfeng bushizi, hebi luan fanshu	清风不识字，何必乱翻书
Qiu Zhijie	邱志杰
qiyun shengdong	气韵生动
qunzhong yundong	群众运动
ren	人
renlei	人类
renwen	人文
Renwen shu	人文书
Rongtai ji	容台集

San zi jing	三字经
shan	山
shi	石
Shijing	诗经
shu ke hui ren, yi ke wu ren	书可慧人，亦可误人
shudaizi	书呆子
shui	水
Song Dong	宋冬
Su Yijian	苏易简
Suyuan shipu	素园石谱
tenghuang	藤黄
tong	桐
Wang Bomin	王伯敏
Wang Jin	王晋
Wei Gao	韦皋
Wei Guangqing	魏光庆
Wenda Gu (Gu Wenda)	谷文达
wenming	文明
wenzi	文字
wenziyu	文字狱
wokou	倭寇
xiangzheng	象征
xianzhuang shu	线装书
xiao hong ren	小红人
Xiaoze Xie (Xie Xiaoze)	谢晓泽
xihua	西画
xijiao	犀角
xingdong de shu	行动的书
Xingxing Huahui	星星画会
Xu Beihong	徐悲鸿
Xu Beihong shengping	徐悲鸿生平
Xu Bing	徐冰
xuanzhi	宣纸
Xue Tao	薛涛
Yang Jiechang	杨诘苍
youhua	油画
Yuan Chin-t'a (Yuan Jinta)	袁金塔
Yue Minjun	岳敏君
yuyi	语意
Zhan Wang	展望
Zhang Daqian	张大千
Zhang Qian	张迁
Zhang Xiaogang	张晓刚
zhen gu zhi dui	鈷故纸堆
Zheng He	郑和
zhu	竹
Zizhi tongjian	资治通鉴

Bibliography

Andrews, Julia F., and Gao Minglu. *Fragmented Memory: The Chinese Avant-Garde in Exile.* Columbus, Ohio: Wexner Center for the Arts, The Ohio State University, 1993.

Beyond the Future: The Third Asia-Pacific Triennial of Contemporary Art. Brisbane: Queensland Art Gallery, 1999.

China's New Art, Post-1989. Hong Kong: Hanart T Z Gallery, 1993.

Clark, John, ed. *Chinese Art at the End of the Millennium: Chinese-art.com 1998–1999.* Hong Kong: New Art Media Ltd., 2000.

______. *Modern Asian Art.* Honolulu: University of Hawaii Press, 1998.

Dreissen, Chris, and Heidi van Mierlo, eds. *Another Long March: Chinese Conceptual and Installation Art in the Nineties.* Breda, The Netherlands: Fundament Foundation, 1997.

Erickson, Britta. *The Art of Xu Bing: Words Without Meaning, Meaning Without Words.* Seattle: University of Washington Press, 2001.

______. *On the Edge: Contemporary Chinese Artists Encounter the West.* Stanford: Iris & B. Gerald Cantor Center for Visual Arts at Stanford University, 2004.

Fan Di'an, Gabriele Knapstein, and Martina Köppel-Yang. *Living in Time: 29 zeitgenössische Künstler aus China.* Berlin: Staatliche Museen zu Berlin, 2001.

Fei Dawei. *Art Chinois: Chine Demain Pour Hier.* Paris: Carte Secrete, 1990.

______. *Cai Guo-Qiang.* New York: Thames and Hudson, 2000.

______. "Two-Minute Wash Cycle: Huang Yong Ping's Chinese Period." In *House of Oracles: A Huang Yong Ping Retrospective,* edited by Philippe Vergne and Doryun Chong. Minneapolis: Walker Art Center, 2005.

The First Academic Exhibition of Chinese Contemporary Art 96–97. Hong Kong: China Oil Painting Gallery Ltd., 1996.

Fumio Nanjo. *Immutability and Fashion: Chinese Contemporary Art in the Midst of Changing Surroundings.* Tokyo: Kirin Brewing Co., Ltd., 1997.

Gao Minglu. "Bawu meishu yundong di 'qianwei' yishi" [The 'avant-garde' consciousness in the '85 art movement]. *Xiongshi meishu* 297 (November 1995), pp. 16–21.

______, ed. *Inside Out: New Chinese Art.* Berkeley: University of California Press, 1998.

______. *The Wall: Reshaping Contemporary Chinese Art.* Buffalo, NY: Albright-Knox Art Gallery, University at Buffalo Art Galleries, 2005.

______. *Zhongguo dangdai meishu shi, 1985–86* [Contemporary art of China]. Shanghai: Shanghai renmin chubanshe, 1991.

Hou Hanru. "Departure Lounge Art: Chinese Artists Abroad." *Art Asia Pacific* 1, no. 2 (April 1994), pp. 36–41.

______. *On the Mid-Ground.* Hong Kong: Timezone 8, 2002.

Hou Hanru, and Hans Ulrich Obrist, eds. *Cities on the Move.* Ostfildern-Ruit, Germany: Verlag Gerd Hatje, 1997.

Huang Yong Ping, "Yishu buxiang zhiwu" [Art – an inauspicious thing]. Quoted in Gao Minglu, *Zhongguo dangdai meishu shi 1985–86,* p. 350.

Huangfu Binghui, ed. *In and Out, Contemporary Art from China and Australia.* Singapore: LaSalle-SIA College of Art, 1997.

Jose, Nicholas, ed. *Mao Goes Pop, China Post-1989.* Sydney: Museum of Contemporary Art, 1993.

Köppel-Yang, Martina. *Semiotic Warfare: A Semiotic Analysis, The Chinese Avant-Garde, 1979–1989.* Hong Kong: Timezone 8, 2003.

Leffingwell, Edward. "Hong Hao at Chambers." *Art in America* 92, no. 6 (June–July 2004), p. 176.

Leng Lin. *It's Me: A Profile of Chinese Contemporary Art in the 90s.* Beijing: Contemporary Art Center Co., 1998.

Li, Xianting. "The Imprisoned Heart: Ideology in an Age of Consumption." *Art and Asia Pacific,* vol. 1, no. 2 (April, 1994), pp. 25–30.

______. "Wuliaogang he 'wenge' hou de disandai yishu jia" [Boredom and Third-Generation Artists in the Post-Cultural Revolution Era], 1991. Quoted in Lü Peng, *Zhongguo dangdai yishushi, 1990–1999* ['90s art China], pp. 95–96.

Lü Peng and Yi Dan. *Zhongguo Xiandai Yishu Shi 1979–1989* [A History of contemporary Chinese art 1979–1989]. Changsha: Hunan Meishu Chubanshe, 1992.

Lü Peng. *Zhongguo Dangdai Yishu Shi, 1990–1999* ['90s art China]. Changsha: Hunan Meishu Chubanshe, 2000.

Noth, Jochen, Wolffer Pöhlmann, and Kai Reschke, eds. *China Avant-garde: Counter-currents in Art and Culture.* Berlin: Haus der Kulturen der Welt, 1994.

Reckoning with the Past: Contemporary Chinese Painting. Edinburgh: Fruitmarket Gallery, 1996.

Rico, Pablo J. "Xu Bing and the 'Well of Truth.'" In *Xu Bing: El Pozo de la Verdad* [The Well of Truth]. Valencia: Sala La Gallera, 2004.

Silent Energy. Oxford: Museum of Modern Art, 1993.

Smith, Karen. *Nine Lives: The Birth of Avant-Garde Art in New China.* Zurich: Scalo, 2005.

Strassberg, Richard E., ed. *"I Don't Want to Play Cards with Cézanne" and Other Works: Selections from the Chinese "New Wave" and "Avant-Garde" Art of the Eighties.* Pasadena, California: Pacific Art Museum, 1991.

Strassberg, Richard E., and Waldemar A. Nielsen. *Beyond the Open Door: Contemporary Paintings from the People's Republic of China.* Pasadena, California: Pacific Art Museum, 1987.

Sullivan, Michael. *The Arts of China.* 3rd ed. Berkeley: University of California Press, 1984.

Wu Hung, ed. *Chinese Art at the Crossroads: Between Past and Present, Between East and West.* Hong Kong: New Art Medium, 2001.

______. *Exhibiting Experimental Art in China.* Chicago: Smart Museum of Art, University of Chicago, 2000.

______, ed. *Reinterpretation: A Decade of Experimental Chinese Art (1999–2000).* Guangzhou: Guangdong Museum of Art, 2002.

______. *Transience: Chinese Experimental Art at the End of the Twentieth Century.* Chicago: Smart Museum of Art, University of Chicago, 1999.

Yang, Alice. *Why Asia? Contemporary Asian and Asian American Art.* New York: New York University Press, 1998.

China Institute Gallery
Exhibitions: 1966–2006

** 1. SELECTIONS OF CHINESE ART FROM PRIVATE COLLECTIONS IN THE METROPOLITAN AREA
November 15, 1966–February 15, 1967
Curator: Mrs. Gilbert Katz

** 2. ART STYLES OF ANCIENT SHANG
April 5–June 11, 1967
Curator: Jean Young

** 3. ANIMALS AND BIRDS IN CHINESE ART
October 25, 1967–January 28, 1968
Curator: Fong Chow

** 4. GARDENS IN CHINESE ART
March 21–May 26, 1968
Curator: Wan-go H.C. Weng

** 5. CHINESE JADE THROUGH THE CENTURIES
October 24, 1968–January 26, 1969
Curator: Joan M. Hartman

** 6. FOREIGNERS IN ANCIENT CHINESE ART
March 27–May 25, 1969
Curator: Ezekiel Schloss

** 7. CHINESE PAINTED ENAMELS
October 23, 1969–February 1, 1970
Curator: J.A. Lloyd Hyde

**8. ALBUM LEAVES FROM THE SUNG AND YUAN DYNASTIES
March 26–May 30, 1970
Curator: C.C. Wang

** 9. MING PORCELAINS: A RETROSPECTIVE
October 29, 1970–January 31, 1971
Curator: Suzanne G. Valenstein

**10. CHINESE SILK TAPESTRY: K'O-SSU
March 24–May 27, 1971
Curator: Jean Mailey

** 11. EARLY CHINESE GOLD AND SILVER
October 21, 1971–January 30, 1972
Curator: Dr. Paul Singer

** 12. DRAGONS IN CHINESE ART
March 23–May 28, 1972
Curator: Hugo Munsterberg

** 13. WINTRY FORESTS, OLD TREES: SOME LANDSCAPE THEMES IN CHINESE PAINTING
October 26, 1972–January 28, 1973
Curator: Richard Barnhart

** 14. CERAMICS IN THE LIAO DYNASTY: NORTH AND SOUTH OF THE GREAT WALL
March 15–May 28, 1973
Curator: Yutaka Mino

** 15. CHINA TRADE PORCELAIN: A STUDY IN DOUBLE REFLECTIONS
October 25, 1973–January 27, 1974
Curator: Claire le Corbeiller

** 16. TANTRIC BUDDHIST ART
March 14–May 24, 1974
Curator: Eleanor Olson

** 17. FRIENDS OF WEN CHENG-MING: A VIEW FROM THE CRAWFORD COLLECTION
October 24, 1974–January 26, 1975
Curators: Marc F. Wilson and Kwan S. Wong

** 18. ANCIENT CHINESE JADES FROM THE | BUFFALO MUSEUM OF SCIENCE
April 3–June 15, 1975
Curator: Joan M. Hartman

** 19. ART OF THE SIX DYNASTIES: CENTURIES OF CHANGE AND INNOVATION
October 29, 1975–February 1, 1976
Curator: Annette L. Juliano

** 20. CHINA'S INFLUENCE ON AMERICAN CULTURE IN THE 18TH AND 19TH CENTURIES
April 8 –June 13, 1976
Curators: Henry Trubner and William Jay Rathburn
(Exhibition traveled to the Seattle Art Museum, October 7–November 28, 1976.)

21. CHINESE FOLK ART IN AMERICAN COLLECTIONS: EARLY 15TH THROUGH 20TH CENTURIES
October 27, 1976–January 30, 1977
Curator: Tseng Yu-Ho Ecke

** 22. EARLY CHINESE MINIATURES
March 16–May 29, 1977
Curator: Dr. Paul Singer

** 23. I-HSING WARE
October 28, 1977–January 29, 1978
Curator: Terese Tse Bartholomew
(Exhibition traveled to the Nelson Gallery of Art, Kansas City, February 19–May 21, 1978, and the Asian Art Museum of San Francisco, June 16–September 21, 1978.)

**24. EMBROIDERY OF IMPERIAL CHINA
March 17–May 28, 1978
Curator: Jean Mailey

** 25. ORIGINS OF CHINESE CERAMICS
October 25, 1978–January 28, 1979
Curator: Clarence F. Shangraw

** 26. ART OF THE HAN
March 14–May 27, 1979
Curator: Ezekiel Schloss

27. TREASURES FROM THE METROPOLITAN MUSEUM OF ART
October 25–November 25, 1979
Curator: Clarence F. Shangraw

** 28. CHINESE ART FROM THE NEWARK MUSEUM
March 19–May 25, 1980
Curators: Valrae Reynolds and Yen Fen Pei

29. CHINESE PORCELAINS IN EUROPEAN MOUNTS
October 22, 1980–January 25, 1981
Curator: Sir Francis Watson

* 30. FREEDOM OF CLAY AND BRUSH THROUGH SEVEN CENTURIES IN NORTHERN CHINA: TZ'U-CHOU TYPE WARES 960–1600 a.d.
March 16–May 24, 1981
Curator: Yutaka Mino
(Exhibition originated at Indianapolis Museum of Art.)

**31. THE ART OF CHINESE KNOTTING
July 29–September 21, 1981
Curator: Hsia-Sheng Chen

**32. MASTERPIECES OF SUNG AND YUAN DYNASTY CALLIGRAPHY FROM THE JOHN M. CRAWFORD JR. COLLECTION
October 21, 1981–January 31, 1982
Curator: Kwan S. Wong, assisted by Stephen Addiss
(Exhibition traveled to the Spencer Museum, University of Kansas, March 14–April 18, 1982.)

33. THE COMMUNION OF SCHOLARS: CHINESE ART AT YALE
March 20–May 30, 1982
Curator: Mary Gardner Neill
(Exhibition traveled to the Museum of Fine Arts, Houston, June 22–August 22, 1982, and the Yale Art Gallery, New Haven, October 5, 1982–April 17, 1983.)

* 34. CHINA FROM WITHIN
November 4–December 12, 1982
A Smithsonian Institution Travelling Services Exhibition, organized by the International Photography Society in cooperation with the China Exhibition Agency, Beijing, and the Chinese Embassy, Washington, DC

**35. BAMBOO CARVING OF CHINA
March 18–May 29, 1983
Curators: Wang Shixiang and Wan-go H.C. Weng
(Exhibition traveled to The Nelson-Atkins Museum of Art, Kansas City, July 24–September 11, 1983, and the Asian Art Museum of San Francisco, October 3, 1983–January 15, 1984.)

36. CHINESE CERAMICS OF THE TRANSITIONAL PERIOD: 1620–1683
October 21, 1983–January 29, 1984
Curator: Stephen Little
(Exhibition traveled to the Kimbell Art Museum, Fort Worth, May 26–August 26, 1984.)

* 37. MASTERPIECES OF CHINESE EXPORT PORCELAIN AND RELATED DECORATIVE ARTS FROM THE MOTTAHEDEH COLLECTION
February 10–March 7, 1984
U.S.–China 200 Bicentennial Exhibition, organized by Anita Christy

**38. CHINESE TRADITIONAL ARCHITECTURE
April 6–June 10, 1984
Curator: Nancy Shatzman Steinhardt
(A permanent travelling exhibition of China Institute. Shown at Allegheny College, Meadeville, PA, March 28–April 19, 1985; Marlboro College, Marlboro, VT, September 11–October 31, 1985; State University of New York, Binghamton, January 7–February 27, 1986.)

** 39. CHINESE RARE BOOKS IN AMERICAN COLLECTIONS
October 20, 1984–January 29, 1985
Curator: Soren Edgren

40. THE SUMPTUOUS BASKET: CHINESE LACQUER WITH BASKETRY PANELS
March 20– June 3, 1985
Curator: James C.Y. Watt

** 41. KERNELS OF ENERGY, BONES OF EARTH: THE ROCK IN CHINESE ART
October 26, 1985–January 26, 1986
Curator: John Hay

* 42. PUPPETRY OF CHINA
April 19–June 29, 1986
Curator: Roberta Helmer Stalberg
Organized by the Center for Puppetry Arts, Atlanta

43. SELECTIONS OF CHINESE ART FROM PRIVATE COLLECTIONS
October 18, 1986–January 4, 1987
Exhibition celebrating the 60th Anniversary of China Institute and the 20th Anniversary of China Institute Gallery, organized by James C.Y. Watt and Annette L. Juliano.

* 44. 1987 NEW YEAR EXHIBITION

* 45. CHINESE FOLK ART
April 4–May 30, 1987
Curator: Nancy Zeng Berliner

** 46. RICHLY WOVEN TRADITIONS: COSTUMES OF THE MIAO OF SOUTHWEST CHINA AND BEYOND
October 22, 1987–January 4, 1988
Curator: Theresa Reilly

* 47. 1988 NEW YEAR EXHIBITION
February 4–February 24, 1988

** 48. RITUAL AND POWER: JADES OF ANCIENT CHINA
April 23–June 19, 1988
Curator: Elizabeth Childs-Johnson

* 49. STORIES FROM CHINA'S PAST
September 17–November 12, 1988
Curator: The Chinese Culture Center of San Francisco

* 50. 1989 NEW YEAR EXHIBITION: LANTERNS
January 28–February 25, 1989

* 51. MIND LANDSCAPES:
THE PAINTINGS OF C.C. WANG
April 3–May 27, 1989
Curator: Jerome Silbergeld

**52. CHINA BETWEEN REVOLUTIONS:
PHOTOGRAPHY BY SIDNEY D. GAMBLE, 1917–1927
June 29–September 9, 1989
Curator: The Sidney D. Gamble Foundation for China Studies and China Institute in America

* 53. VIEWS FROM JADE TERRACE:
CHINESE WOMEN ARTISTS, 1300–1912
October 5–December 2, 1989
Organized by Indianapolis Mùseum of Art

* 54. 1990 NEW YEAR EXHIBITION:
THE CHINESE EARTH–VIEWS OF NATURE
January–March 1990
Curator: Anita Christy

55. CLEAR AS CRYSTAL, RED AS FLAME:
LATER CHINESE GLASS
April 21–June 16, 1990
Curator: Claudia Brown and Donald Robiner

56. THE ECCENTRIC PAINTERS OF YANGZHOU
October 20–December 15, 1990
Curator: Vito Giacalone

* 57. 1991 NEW YEAR EXHIBITION:
CHILDREN IN CHINESE ART
January 26–March 2, 1991
Organized under the auspices of the China Institute Women's Association

**58. ANCIENT CHINESE BRONZE ART:
ASTING THE PRECIOUS SACRAL VESSEL
April 20–June 15, 1991
Curator: W. Thomas Chase

59. EARLY CHINESE CERAMICS FROM
NEW YORK STATE MUSEUMS
October 19–December 14, 1991
Curator: Martie W. Young

60. TREASURES OF THE LAST EMPEROR:
SELECTIONS FROM THE PALACE MUSEUM, BEIJING
February 1–March 7, 1992
Curator: Lawrence Wu

**61. LAMAS, PRINCES AND BRIGANDS:
PHOTOGRAPHS BY JOSEPH ROCK OF THE TIBETAN BORDERLANDS OF CHINA
April 15–July 31, 1992
Curator: Michael Aris

** 62. WORD AS IMAGE:
THE ART OF CHINESE SEAL ENGRAVING
October 21–December 12, 1992
Curator: Jason C. Kuo

63. A YEAR OF GOOD FORTUNE:
LEGENDS OF THE ROOSTER AND TRADITIONS OF THE CHINESE NEW YEAR
January 19–March 6, 1993
Curator: Willow Weilan Hai

* 64. DISCARDING THE BRUSH:
GAO QIPEI, 1660–1734
April 17–June 12, 1993
Curator: Klass Ruitenbeek
Organized by the Rijksmuseum Amsterdam

**65. AS YOU WISH: SYMBOL AND MEANING ON CHINESE PORCELAINS FROM THE TAFT MUSEUM
October 23–January 15, 1994
Curator: David T. Johnson

* 66. SENDING AWAY THE OLD,
WELCOMING THE NEW
February 5–March 5, 1994
Curator: Karen Kane

* 67. CAPTURING A WORLD:
CHINA AND ITS PEOPLE–
PHOTOGRAPHY BY JOHN THOMSON
March 26–June 11, 1994
Curator: organized by the British Council, catalog by the British Council

* 68. AT THE DRAGON COURT:
CHINESE EMBROIDERED MANDARIN SQUARES FROM THE SCHUYLER V.R. CAMMANN COLLECTION
October 20–December 22, 1994
Brochure from similar show which took place at Yale Univ. Art Gallery
Curator: John Finlay

**69. ANIMALS OF THE CHINESE ZODIAC:
CELEBRATING CHINESE NEW YEAR
January 20–March 4, 1995
Curator: Willow Weilan Hai

70. CHINESE PORCELAINS OF THE SEVENTEENTH CENTURY: LANDSCAPES, SCHOLARS' MOTIFS AND NARRATIVES
April 22–August 5, 1995
Curator: Julia B. Curtis

71. ABSTRACTION AND EXPRESSION IN CHINESE CALLIGRAPHY
October 14–December 21, 1995
Curator: H. Christopher Luce
(Exhibition traveled to the Seattle Art Museum, Washington, November 21, 1996 to March 23, 1997.)

* 72. CALLIGRAPHY AS LIVING ART:
SELECTIONS FROM THE JILL SACKLER CHIENSE CALLIGRAPHY COMPETITION
Feburary 3–March 9, 1996
Curator: Willow Weilan Hai, in conjunction with the A. M. Sackler Foundation, Washington, D.C.

* 73. HARE'S FUR, TORTOISESHELL AND PARTRIDGE FEATHERS CHINESE BROWN- AND BLACK-GLAZED CERAMICS, 400–1400
April 20–July 6, 1996
Curator: Robert Mowry
Organized by the Harvard University Art Museum, Massachusetts

74. THE LIFE OF A PATRON: ZHOU LIANGGONG (1612–1672) AND THE PAINTERS OF SEVENTEENTH-CENTURY CHINA
October 23–December 21, 1996
Curator: Hongnam Kim

*75. ADORNMENT FOR ETERNITY: STATUS AND RANK IN CHINESE ORNAMENT
February 6-July 14, 1997
Curators: Julia White and Emma Bunker
Organized by the Denver Art Museum

76. POWER AND VIRTUE: THE HORSE IN CHINESE ART
September 11 - December 13, 1997
Curator: Robert E. Harrist, Jr.

*77. SCENT OF INK: THE ROY AND MARILYN PAPP COLLECTION OF CHINESE ART
February 5 – June 20, 1998
Curator: Claudia Brown
Organized by the Phoenix Art Museum

*78. CHINESE SNUFF BOTTLES FROM THE PAMELA R. LESSING FRIEDMAN COLLECTION
September 16 – December 13, 1998
Organized by the Asian Art Coordinating Council

79. A LITERATI LIFE IN THE TWENTIETH CENTURY: WANG FANGYU—ARTIST, SCHOLAR, CONNOISSEUR
February 11-June 20, 1999
Curator: H. Christopher Luce

80. The Resonance of the Qin in East Asian Art
September 17-December 12, 1999
Curator: Stephen Addiss

*81. The Story of Red: Celebrate the Chinese New Year in 2000
January 12 - February 11, 2000
Curator: Willow Weilan Hai Chang

82. Dawn of the Yellow Earth: Ancient Chinese Ceramics From The Meiyintang Collection
March 21-June 18, 2000
Curator: Regina Krahl

83. The Chinese Painter as Poet
September 14-December 20, 2000
Curator: Jonathan Chaves

*84. LIVING HERITAGE: VERNACULAR ENVIRONMENT IN CHINA
January 25-June 10, 2001
Curator: Kai-yin Lo
Re-organized by the China Institute Gallery

85. EXQUISITE MOMENTS: WEST LAKE & SOUTHERN SONG ART
September 25-December 9, 2001
Curator: Hui-shu Lee

*86. CIRCLES OF REFLECTION: THE CARTER COLLECTION OF CHINESE BRONZE MIRRORS
February 7-June 2, 2002
Curator: Ju-hsi Chou
Organized by the Cleveland Museum of Art

87. Blanc de Chine: Divine Images in Porcelain
September 19–December 7, 2002
Curator: John Ayers

*88. Weaving China's Past: The Amy S. Clague Collection of Chinese Textiles
January 30–June 7, 2003
Curator: Claudia Brown
Organized by the Phoenix Art Museum

89. PASSION FOR THE MOUNTAINS: 17TH CENTURY LANDSCAPE PAINTINGS FROM THE NANJING MUSEUM
September 18 – December 20, 2003
Curator: Willow Weilan Hai Chang

*90. GOLD AND JADE: IMPERIAL JEWELRY OF THE MING DYNASTY FROM THE NANJING MUNICIPAL MUSEUM
February 12 – June 5, 2004
Re-organized by the China Institute Gallery in collaboration with the Nanjing Municipal Museum

*91. THE SCHOLAR AS COLLECTOR: CHINESE ART AT YALE
September 3 – December 11, 2004
Curator: David Ake Sensabaugh
Organized by the Yale University Art Gallery

92. PROVIDING FOR THE AFTERLIFE: "BRILLIANT ARTIFACTS" FROM SHANDONG
February 3 – June 4, 2005
Curators: Susan L. Beningson and Cary Y. Liu
Organized by the China Institute Gallery in collaboration with the Shandong Provincial Museum

*93. MASTERPIECES OF CHINESE LACQUER FROM THE MIKE HEALY COLLECTION
September 16 – December 3, 2005
Curator: Julia M. White
Organized by the Honolulu Academy of Arts

94. TRADE TASTE & TRANSFORMATION: JINGDEZHEN PORCELAIN FOR JAPAN, 1620 – 1645
February 2, 2006 – June 10, 2006
Curator: Julia B. Curtis
Organized by the China Institute Gallery
(Exhibition traveled to the Honolulu Academy of Arts, Honolulu, July 19, 2006 – October 8, 2006)

For information on availability of these titles and others, please contact China Institute in America at (212) 744–8181
* No catalog or exhibition catalog published by another institution
** Catalog out of print

China Institute

FRIENDS OF THE GALLERY

Patrons
Mark Kingdon and Anla Cheng Kingdon
Argie and Oscar Tang

Leaders
Jane DeBevoise and Paul Calello
John R. and Lynne W. Doss
Robert T. and Kay F. Gow
Abel and Sophia Sheng

Sponsors
Susan L. Beningson
John R. and Julia B. Curtis
Dr. Richard and Ruth Dickes
Michael E. and Winnie Feng
Alice King
Margro R. Long
Jeannette N. Rider
Robert Rosenkranz and Alexandra Munroe
Mary J. Wallach
Charlotte C. Weber
Marie-Hélène and Guy A. Weill
Wan-go H.C. Weng
Yvonne L.C. and Frederick Wong

Friends
Christopher J. Ankner and Nancy Yeh-Ankner
Robert M. Beningson
Josephine Berger-Nadler
Berwald Oriental Art
Young Yang Chung
Catherine Gamble Curran
Richard M. and Peggy Danziger
Bruce B. and Ruth Stricker Dayton
Elizabeth Strong De Cuevas
Giuseppe Eskenazi
Hart and Nancy B. Fessenden
Agnes Gund and Daniel Shapiro
Tom and Katia Healy
Karen Hsu
Ta Chun Hsu
René Balcer and Carolyn Hsu-Balcer
Miani Johnson
Virginia A. Kamsky

Yue-Sai Kan
William W. Karatz
Angela H. King
James J. and Helen D. Lally
John Jody and Yue Tao Lee
John M. Leger and Sophie Orloff
Karen Li
William M. Lipton
William E. and Helen Y. Little
Robert W. and Virginia Riggs Lyons
Warren A. Mackey
Clare Tweedy McMorris and Howard McMorris, III
Robert E. and Joyce H. Mims
Mechlin and Valery Moore
Veronica Ogden
William Raiford
Theresa M. Reilly
James and Joanne Quan Reynolds
Diane H. Schafer and Jeffrey Stein
Peter Scheinman and Barbara Giordano
Linda Rosenfield Shulsky
David Solo
Anthony M. Solomon
Martha Sutherland
Charles J. Tanenbaum
Patricia P. Tang
Theow-Huang Tow
Shao F. and Cheryl L. Wang
Laura B. Whitman and Thomas Danziger
Yvonne V. Wong
Denis C. & Kathleen Yang
Laurie and David Y. Ying
Robert P. and Barbara Youngman

Academic

Annette L. Juliano and Joseph L. Geneve
Mrs. Henry H. Weldon

GALLERY COMMITTEE

Virginia A. Kamsky, *Chair*
Yvonne L.C. Wong, *Vice-Chair*

Susan L. Beningson
Claudia Brown
John R. Curtis, Jr.
Agnes Gund
Robert Harrist
Maxwell K. Hearn
Annette Juliano
Diane H. Schafer
David Ake Sensabaugh
Jerome Silbergeld
Marie-Hélène Weill
I. Peter Wolff

CONTEMPORARY ART COMMITTEE

Agnes Gund, *Chair*

Ai Wei-Wei
Cai Guo-Qiang
Barbara Hunt
Chiu-Ti Jansen, Esq.
The Honorable Uli Sigg
Robert Storr
Larry Warsh
I. Peter Wolff
Yvonne L.C. Wong
Wu Hung

GALLERY

Willow Weilan Hai Chang, Director
Pao Yu Cheng, Manager of Art Education (DCTA)
Jennifer Choiniere, Gallery Registrar

DOCENTS

Peggy Hung, Senior Docent
Stephanie Lin, Senior Docent
Roberta Nitka, Senior Docent
Larry Chang
Viviane Chen
Wendy Sung
Pamela Frances Yap

VOLUNTEERS

Mary McFadden
Jeannette N. Rider
Anna-Rose Tykulsker
Jackie Handel
Ann Dillon
Hunter Demos

Photo credits

All images, unless otherwise indicated,
were provided by the lenders and the guest curator.